SUPERPOWER

ISRAEL'S UNSTOPPABLE RISE

GIL WEINREICH

TARGUM PRESS

First published 2016
Copyright © 2016 by Gil Weinreich
All rights reserved
ISBN: 978-1-56871-606-0

Published by
TARGUM PRESS
POB 27515
Jerusalem 91274
editor@targumpublishers.com

Distributed by
Ktav Publishers & Distributors Inc.
527 Empire Blvd.
Brooklyn, NY 11225-3121
Tel: 718-972-5449, 201-963-9524
Fax: 718-972-6307, 201-963-0102
www.ktav.com

Printed in Israel

Dedication

In honor of my father, Michael Weinreich (1928-1999)

Born in Europe amidst the continent's death throes;
raised in Israel amidst the Jewish state's painful rebirth;
he made his home in America, whose freedom and
opportunity he loved,
but he never forgot where he came from, often saying:
"I'm from Tel Aviv, but my heart is in Jerusalem."
Today his son, daughter-in-law and grandchildren merit
to live in his heart's home, Israel's eternal capital.

Contents

CHAPTER ONE
A Holy Army

It is a cool and blustery autumn day on a remote hilltop Israeli military base in the Jordan Valley. Normally one can see deep into Jordanian territory from here but a *hamsin* – a dust storm emanating from Egypt or Sudan – surrounds the base in a pall of rust-colored murk. Amidst the haze, young trainees can be seen practicing *krav maga*, an Israeli practical fighting technique, but when a prominent rabbi arrives to give a talk, the group files into a corrugated metal barracks to listen in.

Guns slung over laps, the group breaks into loud song before the rabbi can get in his first words: "*V'haya machanecha kadosh.*"

These words – "And your [military] camp shall be holy" – come from the Bible (Deuteronomy 23:15) and are the anthem of the Netzach Yehuda battalion present at the base.

The song was apt because Rabbi Yitzchak Bar-Chaim, founder of Netzach, popularly known as Nachal

Chareidi, devoted his talk to what makes the brigade distinct from such highly decorated units as the Givati or
Golani brigades.

His answer was that the group is careful to maintain an abode of moral purity, expounding the preceding
part of the verse which states that God "goes along in the
midst of your camp to rescue you, to deliver your enemy
to you" but that this Divine presence is conditional on an
absence of any immodesty.

Men and women do not serve together, and instead
of fraternizing during the long spells of boredom afflicting soldiers at base, the soldiers have a *beit hamidrash* –
a learning space stocked with holy books on Jewish law
and philosophy.

Indeed, inside that very *beit hamidrash*, a humble
shack on that obscure dusty outpost, stands an ark hous-
ing the Israeli military's most powerful armament – a
secret weapon of immense, indeed world-changing sig-
nificance. At designated times the soldiers remove and
unfurl this unique instrument called a *sefer Torah*, a Torah scroll.

The boys of Netzach Yehuda are unlike the typical
American soldier with bulging muscles and scary tattoos
(even if gentlemanly and courteous in other respects).
Despite the tough job they do of dragging terrorists out
of their hiding places amidst an obstreperous and at
times violently resistant population, these Israeli soldiers
are more likely to be of slight build, often accented by
glasses, freckles, untrimmed beards and earlocks.

But they represent an unmistakable and forceful

trend in Israeli society: the growing Judaization of the Jewish state.

Between Two Mighty Colossuses

Israel is surrounded by two extremely different civilizations: a Western world that is formally Christian though predominantly secular in outlook, and commanding immense material resources; and an Islamic world of abject privation but deep reservoirs of religiosity.

While Europe in the modern era has long been noted for its grand cathedrals filled only by the occasional busloads of photo-snapping tourists, even the more religious U.S. is on a marked path of secularization. A 2015 Pew Research Center survey found a steep drop in religious sentiment among young ("millennial generation") Americans, just half of whom hold to a strong faith compared to 71% of the general adult population.[1]

Even amongst those Westerners who retain a religious outlook, what specifically does that entail? Christianity strongly endorses ideals of compassion, brotherhood and charity, but is not oriented toward specific legal obligations to the same extent as Judaism and Islam. So, for example, while the United States is the world's largest Christian society, most states, and recently the U.S. Supreme Court, have declared that marriage between two men is as legitimate as between a man and a woman, a view completely at odds with Biblical morality. It is not quaint notions of family life, but the force of law and stamp of custom that shape a society's values – and in the West, laws and institutions are hurtling rapidly into a brave new world.

The Islamic world, in contrast, is known more for its law than its compassion. The ISIS terrorist group favors hurling alleged homosexuals off rooftops, videotaping their horrific deaths. Paradoxically, homosexual abuse of boys is widely tolerated in Islamic societies as the Quran's family law injunctions have yet to reach the masses of traditional societies where cruelty is the norm.[2] (Abuse of girls, on the other hand, is not just rampant but religiously sanctioned.[3])

While Westerners are rightly appalled by such barbarism, Islam's strengths must be acknowledged. The Muslim religion puts tremendous stock in demonstrating honor to God – Muslims are required to pray five times a day, to cite one well known example – and social relationships are likewise governed by notions of honor, and its dreaded opposite, shame.[4] The Western world is well aware of Muslim proclivities, indeed, barbarism, in this regard. Witness the "honor" killings of women presumed to have brought shame on their families, or the riotous reaction to Western cartoons deemed insulting to their prophet Mohammed.

While Westerners are unable to relate to this extremism, they should at least arrive at two conclusions. First, they should recognize the cultural fact that many Muslims feel honor-bound to the point even of murder in reaction to circumstances that would inspire Westerners to yawn; and correspondingly, Westerners might reflect on their own deficiencies that keep them from understanding Muslim anger. If Westerners could relate to the level of honor Muslims feel for God and religion, they would take seriously just how great a provocation it is to ridicule their prophet for the sake of entertainment.

None of this is to excuse homicidal rampages. The idea is to take an inventory of the state of the world today. Westerners assume they have greater power because they are focused on their economic, technological and military might.

In the Western imagination, hotheads on the Arab street can shout curses and death threats, but if the need arose, a low-level soldier sitting on a Navy ship could push a button, dispatch a missile and incinerate the impotent demonstrators at will.

But Arabs and Muslims have tremendous powers. First of all, they are numerous. Recent videos available online have captured massive currents of refugees quite literally overrunning European towns and cities. While many are eager to work, Islamic belief provides strong justification for the notion that welfare is merely the tax that *dhimmis* (the second-class legal status of Christians under Islamic rule) owe their true masters.

What's more, the Western world's loose sexual morality is seen as an open invitation to rapacious behavior on the part of many immigrants, with the resulting criminality abetted by Western political correctness whose glorification of the value of tolerance requires concealing unflattering images of Islam.

An investigation in 2014 revealed that police in the British city of Rotherham looked the other way amid mounting evidence that Muslim gangs were involved in raping over 1,400 girls. Police, social workers and ordinary citizens seem not to have noticed anything unusual about pre-teen girls socializing with 30-something men.[5]

With Western missiles falling on Muslim lands and Muslim immigrants descending on Western lands and establishing large communities and institutions therein, adhering to their own Sharia laws; the balance sheet between the two clashing civilizations is much more even than the average Westerner may suspect.

Moral and Material Strength Combined

Nature abhors a vacuum, as the saying goes, and the contest for power is thus never absent. New powers continually enter the stage of history, and aging powers exit it. Man-on-the-street notions of what constitutes wealth and power do not correlate with these comings and goings. Rome was a lean, mean fighting machine when it claimed superpower status, and a colossus bestriding the earth when its decline became irreversible.

What this indicates is that a superpower needs both material *and* spiritual resources. The fact that even a socioeconomically *disadvantaged* American lives better than royalty lived throughout much of history in terms of food, living space and material comforts, should not induce mistaken notions of permanent domination.

Muslims' own strong sense of superiority naturally arises from the feeling that they have a relationship with God, and are dealing with opponents lacking as intimate a connection.

In stark contrast to the Western and Islamic worlds, each imbalanced by the lack of a key component of societal strength, Israel and Judaism possess both law *and* morality; justice *and* compassion; material might *and* moral might.

The young soldiers on that Israeli military base represent an enormous force that the world refuses to recognize, denies and even falsifies.

Indeed, the one thing the Western and Muslim worlds agree upon – as expressed through the United Nations and the world's foreign offices – is Jewish perfidy.

The U.S. State Department's condemnations of building homes in Jewish neighborhoods (they have no problem with homebuilding for Arabs); the European Union's Boycott, Divestment, Sanctions (BDS) obsession; the Vatican's signing of a treaty with the "State of Palestine"; the war, terror and murderous incitement emanating from the Muslim world – all these obsessions serve only to blind the world to the rise of the tiny Jewish state as the world's emerging superpower.

What we will explore in the coming chapters involves no secrets, but may nevertheless come as a revelation to those whose eyes do not yet see.

The Western world remains trapped in an overarching sense of guilt for wealth and power achieved through theft and plunder as much as invention and creativity. The rapacious behavior of Islamic armies on the march today evidence no sense of shame on the part of the militants in their view of what is rightfully theirs.

In contrast, Rabbi Bar-Chaim ended his talk with the soldiers on that hilltop base by quoting the verse (Deuteronomy 13:18) commanding the Jewish army to utterly destroy an idolatrous city: "None of the booty shall cling to your hand...and God will give you mercy and be merciful to you..."

The language is odd, and seemingly redundant. Why must God "give mercy" and "be merciful"? The Torah's insight is that war necessitates violence and that the taking of human life will in the course of nature strip a soldier of his humanity. But by doing God's will – destroying a city that is in essence in open rebellion against God – He will "give mercy," that is, restore Jewish soldiers to their original kind natures.

Not only must the Jewish fighters suppress their natural compassion but they must also not succumb to the natural human drive, especially in war, to snatch the enemies' possessions. It is God's desire that these should be banned utterly because of their association with idolatry.

The rabbi cited the Biblical commentator, *Or Ha-Chaim*, who says that since God deals with people according to the way they deal with others, the reward for the moral restraint of the Jewish army is that God will "be merciful."

By behaving as a holy army, these Jewish soldiers are building up *both* Israel's material and spiritual blessings.

Israel is already well known for the might of its military, but more needs to be understood about the growing strengths of its armed forces as well as all other areas that define a superpower. This also relates to the United States, generally assumed to exemplify a superpower *par excellence* by both Americans and America's enemies alike.

CHAPTER TWO
Superpower Careers: Shorter Than You Think

The revolutions that rocked Central and Eastern Europe in the fall of 1989 rejiggered the geopolitical chessboard that had dominated the world since the end of the Second World War. The tearing down of the Berlin Wall that November brought down the entire Iron Curtain that had subdued whole populations for a generation.

Anyone then wondering what the effective disappearance of one of the two superpowers would mean for international security didn't have to wait long to find out. Several months later, Iraqi dictator Saddam Hussein occupied and annexed Kuwait, declaring it an Iraqi province.

The world's remaining superpower, the U.S., responded quickly to defend Kuwait and protect neighboring Saudi Arabia and its massive oil fields from further Iraqi predation. The U.S. amassed an impressive array of air, sea and land forces in the Persian Gulf while simultaneously building diplomatic support through a coalition of 34 countries. While the U.S. military did most of the fighting, UN and international approval and participation were secured in order to establish moral and legal legitimacy for the U.S. intervention.

In a swift military campaign that took place in January and February of 1991, U.S. General "Stormin' Norman" Schwarzkopf expelled the Iraqi occupiers from Kuwait, and, in a ground operation lasting just 100 hours, pushed the Iraqis to within 150 miles of Baghdad.

The Western world's main source of oil was secured, as were the Saudi and Kuwaiti monarchies. But above all, U.S. power and prestige were profoundly enhanced and no one doubted American superpower status. Indeed, the French, long vocal in their criticism of U.S. power throughout its superpower days, now took to calling America a "hyperpower."

When President George H.W. Bush awarded the Presidential Medal of Freedom to Schwarzkopf and General Colin Powell soon after the conclusion of the First Persian Gulf War (or "Desert Storm," as the operation was popularly known), he assessed the meaning of all that had just occurred, as follows:

"Desert Storm marked the end of an era of self-doubt and lingering uncertainty about America's staying power and sense of purpose. Under your leadership, America sent its sons and daughters to confront an enemy abroad, and in the process, you transformed a Nation here at home. Desert Storm dispelled all doubt: America is, and

America always will be, a force for good in the world."[6]

It is painful to have to point out how utterly untrue the president's words were, though there should be no doubt about his sincerity in saying them. After all, as a former Congressman, U.S. ambassador to the UN, head of the Republican National Committee, and ambassador to China, no one had a more panoramic view of how bitterly divided the nation had become during the Vietnam War, and for years afterward.

The excitement in America at that time was indeed palpable; one felt the pride, but it was to be short-lived, as Bush, at the zenith of presidential popularity, would find out just one year later when facing re-election and losing to Bill Clinton amidst a sluggish economy.

Let's size up Bush's words one quarter-century later:

Today, it would be more accurate to state that America, led by Barack Obama, is plagued by self-doubt as well as profound *international* doubt by friends and enemies alike, about its staying power and sense of purpose. Moreover, the cost of America's intervention in Iraq multiplied as the decades wore on, while its apparent successes were transformed into staggering reversals. Further, America as a nation was not "transformed" (perhaps "restored" is the sentiment Bush really had in mind) into a patriotic people sharing a common vision of its role in the world; rather, it became ever more bitterly divided. Finally, the current view of what it means to be a "force for good" is in many respects the opposite of what Bush might have had in mind, particularly since America's foreign policy has been transformed into one in which America is solicitous of its enemies and disdainful of its friends.

One might protest that, nevertheless, America remains the single most powerful country in the world!

The Russians, Chinese and Iranians are challenging the U.S. across the globe; ISIS is running at least a quarter of Iraq and President Barack Obama's red line in Syria is the blood that has spilled since he failed to carry through on his commitment to stop its dictator Bashir Assad; the Republican and Democratic parties agree on nothing to the point of unprecedented political paralysis; and the current administration spits at its friends and mollycoddles the bad guys Even so, you might say, new leadership will change all this and restore America's role in the world.

It's a nice thought, and commonly expressed, but restoring America's greatness is not like flicking on a light switch. Since the time George H.W. Bush offered his paean to America's renewed greatness, four presidents, two of each party – Bush and his son, and Clinton and Obama – have governed, and the trend line has only continued to descend.

Vanishing Superpowers

Americans can, and definitely should, do their utmost to change course, but if it were better understood precisely what a superpower is, it would be clearer that this entails swimming against the tide in a vast ocean. Currently, Israel appears alone in swimming with the current and its small size is irrelevant to its superpower future, as will be explained.

So, let's try to understand what a superpower is. Academics offer a variety of definitions. Some look at the resources a country commands: Does it exercise effective control over a large land mass that is defensible and well defended? Does it have a large population that can man a formidable army? Does it have access to vital commodities such as oil or natural gas, or arable land in the country that can supply its cities?

Others look more at the obvious, external effects of these internal attributes: can the country project its military power abroad? Does its economy cast a shadow over the decisions of other countries? Can it wield influence diplomatically?

Others consider a country's cultural influence, its relative independence, its social coherence or whether it has a unifying ideology.

Certainly, by any historical measure, the U.S. has excelled in most of these areas. However, one should be cautious about reposing excessive confidence in any combination of these qualities, however solid they may appear, since history shows that an apparently unshakeable position can quite quickly and definitively be shaken.

Take the British empire, which after World War II controlled a quarter of the world's population and a quarter of the world's land mass, as well as being an economic and military superpower, and whose recent credits included defeating Nazi Germany.

Yet only a few short years later, Britain buckled as a superpower when in 1956 the U.S. commanded its British cousins to back off from its campaign to oust Gamel Abdel Nasser after the Egyptian dictator nationalized the Franco-British Suez Canal.

Ironically, the British and French undertook that operation in conjunction with Israel, but in history's great drama, Israel's resource-constrained armed forces achieved all of its objectives, foreshadowing the young country's future prowess – even while its defeat of Egyptian forces in the Sinai was obscured at the time by the diplomatic dimming of once great Britain and France.

The new U.S. superpower essentially shoved the Brits off the stage of history by threatening to sell the U.S. Treasury's portfolio of sterling, placing tremendous pressure on the pound at a time of extreme economic vulnerability for a country still recovering from the ravages of war. Interestingly, the British considered occupying Kuwait as a response to threats of U.S. oil sanctions, before deciding to simply back down.

The U.S. could elbow aside the U.K. because it had not suffered massive industrial destruction of its homeland or staggering population losses like its World War II ally; indeed that great global conflict had seen the U.S. *gain* strength relative to the rest of the world, becoming a powerhouse militarily, and, in the economic sphere both the largest creditor nation and seller of goods worldwide.

What's more, U.S. sidelining of Britain was not animated by lingering resentment of colonial repression under King George III. There was probably never greater mutual sympathy among allied nations who had fought alongside one another against Nazi Germany. No, the U.S. was responding to the new threat of the Soviet Union's imperial and ideological ambitions.

In other words, the U.S. answered history's door knock by forming a global strategy meant to contain Communist expansion and uphold a liberal world order, but the completion of that mission should be as terrifying as it is satisfying because the lack of a clear purpose is tantamount to the dimming of the lights that afflict the very old.

Let's take a *quick* inventory of America's current preeminence according to various criteria of superpower status, saving more detailed discussion for the chapters ahead.

Economically, the U.S., the largest creditor nation after World War II, is today the largest debtor nation.

Militarily, U.S. power is contracting to the point where America has undone its hard-won victories in Iraq and Afghanistan, has left a power vacuum that its former enemy Russia is filling in Eastern Europe and Syria, has ceded its supremacy in Asia, and has even effectively lost control of its own southern border.

Diplomatically, the U.S. has worked long and hard, even exhaustively – making that extra push when failure seemed at hand on numerous occasions – to conceive, nurture and empower its most important geopolitical challenger by crowning Iran with nuclear weapons capability.

U.S. ideology today – from the White House to the schoolhouse – centers on fighting global warming. In a recent major policy address to the U.S. Coast Guard,

President Obama told graduating cadets that combatting climate change will be amongst the U.S. military's most important duties. Fighting imagined enemies, while letting real ones with murderous ambitions ensconce themselves, augurs poorly for future superpower status.

Culturally, a recent Gallup survey[7] tracking American attitudes toward moral issues found that in *every* area these attitudes have moved in a more liberal direction, and that the biggest shift of all is in the acceptance of gay and lesbian relationships. As we'll see, the rejection of time-honored universal moral standards is corrosive of society's foundations and, as such, incompatible with superpower status.

We will examine America's profound shifts in these key correlates of power, while describing the surprising emergence of Israel, quietly building strengths – oddly undetected or unacknowledged – in all these areas.

The U.S. remains globally dominant to be sure, but it is a mistake to take preeminence for permanence. Already three superpowers – Nazi Germany, Britain and Soviet Russia – got knocked out in the lifespans of many still around today.

CHAPTER THREE
What's the Point of West Point?

Author and speaker Rabbi Benjamin Blech tells the story of a non-religious Jewish military cadet who took a required course in military strategies at West Point, examining famous battles throughout history. The cadet, bothered that the case studies did not include the wars between Israel and the Arab states, raised his hand and asked the teacher about this omission. Rather than answer the question, the general ordered the cadet to meet him in his office after class.

As told by the cadet's rabbi, a friend of Blech's, who was shocked to see him return from West Point garbed in religious attire, the young man related how the general's response inspired his return to tradition:

"Young man! The greatest military strategists in the world have examined, dissected and analyzed the wars that Israel has fought and won. No matter how you look at it, they should have lost every single time. It is perfectly clear that it was not their weapons or their strength or the strategies that they used that gave victory to Israel.

The only reason that can honestly explain Israel's victories is that they are miracles – and at West Point Military Academy we do not teach miracles."[8]

It's a cute story. But the reality is that Israel *did* win those wars. So West Point and the world's other military strategists must reckon with this reality. What's the point of political or strategic analysis that omits a part of reality that most people have no trouble acknowledging in their churches, mosques or homes? If mathematicians can solve for x, military analysts should make sure their strategic equations account for m (miracle).

That said, whatever Divine assistance Israel's military receives is concealed. Look closely at the miracles described in the Hebrew Bible and you will see that they are all performed under cover of natural means. An all-powerful God could certainly command the parting of the Sea of Reeds so the Israelites fleeing Egypt could escape the Egyptian army, but instead, God commands a wind to blow *all* night long to build the strength to part the waters naturally. Even then, the waters parted only when the first Israelite entered the sea's raging waters.

And so it is with the Israel Defense Forces, whose remarkable performance is proportionate to the initiative it has shown. The IDF has earned a reputation the world over as a highly effective military organization: battle-hardened; technologically advanced; a citizen army with genuine *esprit de corps*; and a long track record of success. This is a military which in 1976, fewer than 30 years since its formation, managed to project its power beyond its immediate region to rescue Israeli citizens held hostage by Palestinian terrorists in Entebbe, Uganda.

That same military, just five years later, took out Iraq's Osirak nuclear installation. The move was condemned by the whole world, including the United States, though it is doubtful the U.S. would have had any good options in confronting a nuclear Iraq just 10 years later without the Jewish state's daring move. Had Israel not destroyed Syria's budding nuclear program in 2007, those nukes would today be in the hands of the regime's brutal dictator Bashar al-Assad or ISIS, in either case severely burdening U.S. options in the region.

Given the IDF's lethal reputation, and its constant presence in the news, one might be forgiven for not knowing that Israel's army is not even in the top 20 largest armed forces worldwide or that it is less than half the size of Colombia's. Despite the fact that Israel's enemies have launched or provoked every single one of the wars it has fought, the IDF has gone further than any military in history in minimizing casualties of its opponent's civilian population.

These large and frequent victories for a small and constantly beleaguered army lend immediate credence to the West Point general's comment, and one which the IDF's soldiers themselves would not dispute. It seems that every soldier has his own personal observations of inexplicable successes or averted failures.

Defeatism and Dementia

The U.S. military functions on an entirely different scale from the IDF, which does not possess even a single aircraft carrier. The United States is the only military power with capabilities that span the entire world, and it has generally dominated every region therein, though in recent years the Chinese military has gradually stepped up its attempts to achieve primacy within Asia. The training that U.S. military recruits endure, especially Marines, is probably second to none in its physical demands, and military discipline is strong. While the U.S. military has repeatedly won the respect of its international opponents, it bears mentioning that perhaps, even more crucially, the U.S. military is respected at home. At a time when many American institutions, especially governmental ones, lack that respect, Americans and their elected representatives generally admire and support U.S. servicemen and veterans.

And yet, despite all these strengths, one sees that U.S. military power worldwide is indeed contracting, and U.S. enemies today hold sway in areas such as Iraq, where the U.S. has expended tremendous amounts of blood and financial resources over the past quarter-century. The terrorist group, ISIS, for example, has taken advantage of U.S. passivity in Syria and now dominates a majority of the country's territory (albeit the least populated parts of it), while other terrorists, including the Damascus-based regime, divide up other parts of the war-torn country. Libya is also divided up by various terrorist groups after the U.S. and a multinational invasion force destabilized the country for no discernable strategic purpose. Iraq is similarly fragmented by various groups, including ISIS and a weak Iranian-influenced central government, as well as moderate Kurds whom Washington has failed to support fully.

In Asia, China has built facts on the ground – literally, through land reclamation projects in the South

China Sea; on the sea, through naval power that now exceeds in quantity the combined number of vessels of the U.S. and its Asian allies; and in the air, having unilaterally declared a defense zone over islands controlled by Japan, Taiwan and South Korea, which China is quite aggressively patrolling. U.S.-China tension has been steadily increasing in these areas, and China continually demonstrates that it does not intend to back down.

Perhaps most alarming of all, the U.S. seems to have lost control of its own southern border. In 2014, Marine Corps General John Kelly, head of the U.S. Southern Command, gave testimony before Congress in which he said that budget cuts were "severely degrading" his efforts to stop illegal approaches to the border, adding that his forces are unable to act on 75% of illicit trafficking events. "I simply sit and watch it go by," he said. That "it" referred not only to drug gangs but to Hezbollah and even potential weapons of mass destruction. In an interview with the journal *Defense One*, Kelly had this to say[9]:

"All this corruption and violence is directly or indirectly due to the insatiable U.S. demand for drugs, particularly cocaine, heroin and now methamphetamines," a subject we will address in Chapter 6.

Kelly concluded his testimony before the House Armed Services Committee with a sharp observation about his Southern Command that could equally apply across the globe[10]:

"Some of my [Latin American] counterparts perceive that the United States is disengaging from the region and from the world in general. We should remember that our friends and allies are not the only ones watching our actions closely. Reduced engagement could itself become a national security problem, with long-term, detrimental effects on U.S. leadership, access, and interests in a part of the world where our engagement has made a real and lasting difference. And in the meantime, drug traffickers, criminal networks, and other actors, unburdened by budget cuts, cancelled activities, and employee furloughs, will have the opportunity to exploit the partnership vacuum left by reduced U.S. military engagement."

The U.S. military is surely one of the most impressive fighting forces in history. Its record of achievement spans the centuries. No doubt its troops can do more push-ups than their foreign counterparts. General Kelly's comments evince the wisdom of an experienced soldier. So why is it that America's adversaries from Russia to China to ISIS perceive that the United States "is disengaging… from the world," and have acted to "exploit the vacuum left by reduced U.S. military engagement"?

Numerous explanations can be supplied to answer this question. The government's own National Intelligence Council, in its most recent national intelligence estimate, offered over 100 pages' worth in an assessment projecting a rapid decline in U.S. power by 2030: "The 'unipolar moment' is over and Pax Americana…is fast winding down," it concluded.[11]

A single, simple observation well describes the trend of the past quarter-century, and regardless of which party has held power: To wit, there is no war that America's soldiers can win that its politicians and diplomats are unprepared to lose.

By politicians and diplomats, we also include the most senior military officers above the combatant commands. These are politically ambitious types who know how to assuage their political masters in Washington even if that means defying the simple common sense by which soldiers live or die.

To cite an illustrative example, in the second phase of the U.S.-Iraq war during the administration of George W. Bush, the biggest factor accounting for as much as two-thirds of U.S. and allied force deaths, were the improvised explosive devices (I.E.D.s). Any ordinary American reading the newspaper understood that Iranians were supplying the insurgents with these devices or the know-how to make them.

At first blush, this might not have made sense to U.S. military strategists. After all, the U.S. was fighting and weakening Iran's chief rival, Iraq, so the Iranians should have been happy to have America do its dirty work for them. But somehow U.S. policy makers have failed to grasp that in the big picture rather than the local theater of conflict, Iran views the United States as its chief rival. They have taken U.S. diplomats hostage, they shout "Death to America" in daily public hate rituals – but none of this has quite gotten through to American policy makers.

America's lethal military force was already on the ground right next door to Iran and could have exacted a high price – up to and including revenge for the humiliation of the 1979-81 U.S. hostage crisis, for Iran's leading role in killing U.S. troops. But America's timorous leadership, perhaps sensitive to the unpopularity of the Iraq war, was reluctant to expand the mission, even though doing so could have assured it of victory in Iraq while addressing the biggest source of instability in the region. Iran at that time was weak and fearful of U.S. power, though bold in stealthily seeking to undermine American support for the war by increasing the number of body bags returning to the U.S.

This *New York Times'* lead paragraph from February 2007 typified the Socratic U.S. approach to Iranian IEDs[12]:

"A raid on a Shiite weapons cache in the southern city of Hilla one week ago is providing what American officials call the best evidence yet that the deadliest roadside bombs in Iraq are manufactured in Iran, but critics contend that the forensic case remains circumstantial and inferential."

The article makes for painful reading. It quotes the top U.S. military explosives expert who recounted a long list of technical indicators pointing to the weapons' Iranian provenance, including the components, the sophistication of their manufacture and the fact that similar explosive devices were also only found in the Levant – in use by Iran's client Hezbollah.

But, as the *Times* framed the story: critics pointing to "the flawed intelligence used by the administration to accuse Saddam Hussein of harboring unconventional weapons, before invading Iraq" were looking for U.S. courtroom-style evidence perhaps available only after years of resolving doubts, an accumulation of dead soldiers, and a lost war.

The defeatist mentality that prevails in U.S. universities, where Republicans and Democrats alike are educated, and that permeates the U.S. media's conversations about the issues of the day, ensures that America's leadership will behave in ways that do not comport with common sense.

Indeed, the turning point of the American hyperpower's first unipolar strategic challenge discussed in the previous chapter came about after the fall of the Soviet Union. The unprecedented decision of the government of George H.W. Bush to seek United Nations support, and to build an international coalition whose troops were not really needed marked a sea change in US international behavior. The only question should have been whether the war served U.S. national interests, and whether the U.S. public, through its elected representatives, would see it as such.

In making this disastrous decision, Bush gave power over U.S. decisions to Burundi and Slovenia (and a plethora of other countries whose counsel was not needed), and more fatally, elevated global opinion above considerations of U.S. national interests.

Fast-forward to today. The Iranians exercise immense geopolitical power. Worse, the administration of Barack Obama has cravenly appeased Tehran with an agreement that creates a clear path to nuclearization.

Common sense alone would suggest that the Iranians are up to no good, as they have all the fossil-fuel energy they could ever want without any need to invest in "peaceful" nuclear energy. Perhaps the president is so profound an environmentalist that in his eyes the Iranians are admirably "going green;" or he places his faith in inspections efforts, despite the failure of inspections – or U.S. resolve – as applied to Iraqi or North Korean programs in recent years.

Maybe the greatest indication of the growing dementia in U.S. policy circles came with the (minimally covered) news story in November 2015 - the U.S. State Department actually admitted in response to a query by U.S. Congressman, Mike Pompeo, that the Iranians didn't even bother to sign the hard-defended nuclear deal with the U.S.[13] Yes, you read that correctly.

By the way - why has the U.S. devoted years of arduous negotiations with Iran to curb its nuclear weapons development program when the Iranians already obligated themselves, and remain obligated, to not develop such weapons under the international Nuclear Non-Proliferation Treaty Iran signed in 1968?

Clearly, the Iranians don't mind lying and violating agreements. They probably couldn't believe the U.S. would accede to their patently unreasonable objections to signing what to them was just a stack of paper anyway. Most likely, the U.S. negotiating team, tired of every last minor roadblock the Iranians kept throwing their way, simply gave up in order to meet some artificial deadline set in Washington. Photos of the diplomats posing at what we now know to be a non-signing ceremony, showed the Iranian negotiators laughing hysterically next to their bemused-looking Western counterparts. [14]

Indeed, they were right to do so. Within months of

the July 2015 non-signing ceremony, the Iranians tested ballistic missiles, in October and again in December, in flagrant violation of their assumed legal obligations, and with no meaningful repercussions from Washington.[15]

The large and omni-competent U.S. military can defeat its foes the world over, but is no match for feeble-minded U.S. foreign policy and media elites.

A Few Good Men

The Israeli military is much, much smaller. It too can handle any combination of its Middle Eastern enemies, though currently it too is overpowered by its defeatist politicians (including the highest-ranking politicized generals and intelligence chiefs), diplomats, media and academic critics. But, as will be discussed in Chapter 6, Israeli society is moving countercyclically with Western societies. Its depressed elite is shrinking, and the patriots are gaining ground. More importantly, the Israeli military does not need large troop numbers to win its wars.

The Biblical story of Gideon shows that the Israeli military, then and now, is more interested in quality than quantity (Judges, Chapter 7). Facing a quantitatively superior force of 135,000 Midianites, Gideon actually *reduced* his meager troop of 32,000 volunteers, first to 10,000, then to just 300. These men were selected strictly on the basis of character; Gideon had them go down to the river to drink water, and chose those who lifted the water to their mouths in a dignified manner rather than put their heads into the water like an animal.

The 300 snuck into the enemy camp in the middle

of the night, armed with shofars (ram's horns), torches and jugs. They put their torches in their jugs, blew on their shofars making a loud noise, then smashed their jugs with the lit torches inside, revealing brilliant flames amidst the frightening sound. An army normally has one bugler and torch bearer, so these few men convinced the Midianites they were part of an enormous army. Gideon's army had surrounded the camp on three sides, leaving just one escape route, obligingly taken by the Midianites in their desperate maneuvers to escape.

This story demonstrates the value of military shrewdness by which a numerically inferior force can frighten its opponents, as well as the importance of giving the enemy an alternative to fighting (i.e. the single escape route). Unlike that general at West Point, Israeli military trainers mine Biblical stories, like that of Gideon, in their officer training. But perhaps the most potent lesson of the story of how 300 men defeated an army of 135,000 is that under the veneer of real-world strategy and tactics lies a non-natural source of victory.

CHAPTER FOUR
A Brittle Juggernaut vs. a Little Jug with a Lot

In 2008, global financial markets plunged, and major U.S. financial institutions verged on collapse were it not for the ungraspable sum of $24 trillion in actual or pledged support by the U.S. government.[16] At that time, representatives of the U.S. private banking office of Israel's Bank Leumi approached a kippah-wearing journalist attending the same financial conference in Miami, hoping for an explanation of what was going on.

With incomprehension written on their faces, they exclaimed that they might have expected a crisis of such proportions in other parts of the world, but the U.S.? They noted, without pride (the crisis was adversely affecting their southern Florida-based clientele, and thus their own business), that even Israeli banks were holding up just fine.

This author didn't have a particularly articulate reply to their query at the time, but it is worth highlighting a significant detail that remains a mere footnote in the midst of the most severe financial crisis since the Great Depression: Israel was a rare island of stability amid continents of volatility.

Sure, traders in Tel Aviv also dumped stocks and bonds, but Israel's banks were strong and stable, its capital markets unexposed to complex derivative instruments whose cancerous malignancy spread between U.S. financial institutions and their international correspondents.

The Israeli economy's financial crisis performance was not merely the result of positive cyclical factors, as economists are wont to discuss, but derived from a deeper structural strength, including sound fiscal and monetary policies, balance of payment surpluses, high foreign exchange reserves, above-average economic growth, low unemployment, and critically, low household debt.[17]

Unusually, perhaps even uniquely, the safety of Israel's economic and market structure does not come at the expense of economic profit; rather, it enhances it.

The Jewish state has earned a worldwide reputation as the "Start-Up Nation." Dan Senor and Saul Singer's book of the same name details how such a small country attracts more than twice as much venture capital on a per-person basis as the U.S., and 30 times as much as Europe.

Similarly, it's fairly well known that large multinational corporations conduct much of their R&D work in Israel. Intel, HP, IBM, Cisco, Microsoft, Google, Apple, and the list goes on – employ tens of thousands of Israelis. They're in Israel because, as Intel Israel's president told a Tel Aviv tech conference in late 2015: "Israel is crucial to Intel. Intel cannot do without the geniuses here in Israel."[18]

Entrepreneurial risk-taking is alive and well in Israel – no other place in Asia or Europe comes close. It's a market with a long upside. Since every business cycle includes downturns, Israel's superior capacity to withstand asset price declines must be reckoned a supreme advantage in today's overleveraged global economy.

This chapter will not rehash the well told story of Israel's high-tech, high-growth economy, nor belabor the less well known story of its well-regulated economic foundation. At any given time there are surely faster-growing economies. International investors in recent decades have salivated over China's vast market and high growth, and would surely scoff at the notion that Israel's relatively small market and merely above-average growth rate should merit their attention.

Similarly, at any given time, there may also be a few advanced economies sporting more conservative debt-to-GDP levels and the like. Currency traders worried about U.S. or European fiscal policies often load up on Swiss francs, and are not likely to view the Israeli shekel as an alternative safe haven for their wealth.

Long after China implodes, as it currently seems set to do, or the strengthening Swiss franc leads consumers to Belgian chocolate and Japanese watches (when their Swiss counterparts become too expensive), Israel's deep economic strengths are likely to lead it to new, and unexpected, heights.

Consider: the country whose products make your cell phones so smart, only a few decades ago was best known for kibbutzim-grown oranges. From a 1950s-era economy based on light industry, agriculture and German war reparations, combined with bond purchases and philanthropy from North American Jews, today's Israel outranks France, Austria and Belgium in the UN's Human Development Index, and as such is considered very highly developed.

Historians who study what is termed "development economics" are particularly interested in the disparate outcomes of countries that were once peers. A classic World Bank case study compared Ghana and South Korea, whose GDPs were roughly the same in 1957, seeking to understand why the latter's per capita purchasing power was about 10 times that of the former just 30 years later. A similar, though less dramatic divergence, was seen between the U.S. and Argentina before the onset of the 20th century.

An academic study[19] that has looked at Israel through this lens shows that the Jewish state has substantially surpassed all but one of its 1953-era developing nation peers (including Chile and Ireland), with only Japan's per capita GDP outpacing Israel's. Don't bet on that advantage lasting, for reasons we will now begin to explain.

A Powerhouse...of Cards

But let's focus on the U.S., the world's acknowledged economic superpower, whose economy is stronger than Japan's and Europe's. We'll largely shy away from numbers and statistics, instead painting a simple word-picture to make this discussion more digestible to those who do not follow the economy and markets professionally.

In the big picture, the economy, boiled down to its essence, is a picture of the flow of money. In recent years, credit and money have flowed out of proportion to the production of the economic actors in actuality. If this is correct, it would seem to follow that balance will eventually be restored to the world's financial horizons through a harsh corrective shrinking.

Specifically, the most recent global economic crisis began in the fall of 2007 with the discovery that toxic "subprime loans" were circulating at unknown addresses through the U.S. financial system. The immediate cause of infection of the financial system stemmed from banks that were selling loans to non-creditworthy customers, then packaging these loans into debt securities and selling them far and wide as mortgage bonds.

(The longer-term cause of the problem: Washington used its outsized influence over the mortgage market through quasi-governmental loan guarantors, Fannie Mae and Freddie Mac, to induce banks to lend to financially unqualified borrowers. As a result, the politicians got the votes, Wall Street got the money and ordinary Americans lost more than $19 trillion in household wealth while the world financial system nearly collapsed.)

In a desperate attempt to stave off a second Great Depression, the Federal Reserve, America's central bank, began lowering interest rates, at around 5% in the fall of 2007, achieving an unprecedented near-zero rate by the end of 2008. The purpose of this policy – which is essentially a form of money printing – is to encourage economic actors to invest in riskier assets that have a potentially positive return, such as the stocks and bonds of U.S. businesses.

It is doubtful that any of the architects of this emergency response could imagine that eight years later the U.S. economy would remain dependent on this form of financial steroids. The Federal Reserve makes headlines in each of its bi-monthly policy meetings where it discusses a withdrawal of central bank support for the economy. Financial commentators are on the news daily, offering their predictions of the timing of such a move. But, while it has been discussed and predicted earnestly and with conviction, it took seven full years for the Fed to make the tiniest gesture (a quarter-of-a-percent rate hike) in the direction of non-emergency monetary policy!

Moving away from monetary to fiscal policy – that is, the realm of spending and taxes determined by politicians in the White House and Congress – it is well known that the federal government spends in excess of tax revenues year in and year out. This governmental overspending enables the population at large to enjoy a higher standard of living than is strictly accounted for by our productivity as a nation.

Where does all this money that makes up for our overspending come from? It is well known that high levels of savings by foreigners, mostly in Asia, have aided high levels of consumption in the U.S. Less well known, is that China has been paring down its ownership of U.S. debt as it spends more to stimulate its own rapidly decelerating economy.

China's rapid growth was a godsend during the last economic crisis, its vast surpluses compensating for contraction the world over. But for the foreseeable future, China is no longer in the double-digit GDP growth league. Economic growth has slowed to a 7% annual rate according to official statistics, though many independent China watchers are convinced that growth has sunk to the low, maybe even very low, single digits.

While the Japanese are once again the top buyers of our bonds, no entity in the history of the world has ever printed more money, relative to the size of its economy, than the Bank of Japan is currently doing, so it's hard to take comfort in this. It's like having your credit-stressed brother pay off your credit card debt with his own credit card, while neither party has realistic prospects of achieving solvency.

The point of all this dismal discussion is to highlight the reality that the economic model of the world's leading superpower does not meaningfully differ from that of Greece, which news followers understand to be an essentially bankrupt country.

Of course, the Greek economy is smaller and weaker than that of the U.S., but the model is the same. The Greeks were living far beyond their means, and after years of agonizing negotiations and debt rescheduling, their European (mainly German) creditors demanded (and got) terms that allowed EU administrators in Brussels to make fiscal choices for the Greek people in return for bailout money.

One might take comfort in the fact that the U.S. is

bigger and stronger than Greece. But *discomfort* is the more sensible reaction – for who in the world has the resources to bail out the U.S., in the way financially constrained Europeans did for the Greeks?

One might say: We will eventually grow our way out of our debt. That was a controversial position back in the 1980s, but there's no need to wade into Reaganomics now. Sources of growth have dried up. The population has aged; family sizes have shrunk; technological innovation has not been at the level of the railroad or computer revolution; Twitter has not unleashed a wave of productivity.

Worse, the financial bankruptcy that could ensue if America's creditors come calling in a crisis seems linked to a certain moral bankruptcy evident in U.S. economic policy.

"Pride comes before the fall," as the saying (Proverbs 16:18) goes. A symptom of pride is complacency. Remember the $787 billion "stimulus" program of 2009? Who can name some lasting achievements from that unprecedented expenditure? Did it accomplish sustained U.S. economic growth? A near trillion dollars is a lot of money to scatter in the wind, even for a country as fabulously rich as the United States.

Despite America's vast wealth, the U.S. neglects real needs in education, infrastructure and national security while vainglorious politicians fritter away the money.

The Federal Reserve, with its immense power and prestige, is hoping the economy will somehow ignite – which it has failed to do despite policies akin to throwing money out of helicopters. The U.S. central bank may be helpless if a force beyond its control triggers a renewed economic crisis.

Will it be the fall of a financial institution like Lehman in the last crisis, or the fall of a weapon of mass destruction from a North Korean or Iranian ICBM, whose offensive capabilities administrations of both parties have failed to forestall? Perceiving weakness, America's enemies are actively testing U.S. resolve and finding it wanting. (These issues will be further discussed in Chapter 7.)

Whatever the precipitating cause, the U.S. has relatively less wherewithal to combat the next crisis. With interest rates at near zero and a seven-year hiatus before the Fed inched them up, they cannot be credibly or meaningfully cut - despite former Fed chair Ben Bernanke's assurances about unspecified "tools" in policymakers' "toolkits".There is no fast-growing large-sized economy like China to pick up the economic slack when the advanced economies' soft underbelly is again exposed.There is no other guarantor of international security when China, Russia, Iran, North Korea or ISIS menace U.S. interests. (Let's be candid – ISIS has more relevance as a state than Greece or many other countries can claim)

America has had years to prepare for the next financial or military crisis, but has failed to do so. For example, the biggest banks today hold a bigger share of the U.S. economy than they had in 2007-08, despite massive and intrusive regulations specifically designed to end "too big to fail" financial institutions. U.S. armed forces, and the shadow America casts internationally, have shrunk considerably in that time as well.

England once experienced a similar, though lesser, decline in the years preceding World War II. It took a Winston Churchill to shore up the island nation in a spectacular burst of glory, for a few years anyway, before Britain resumed its decline. Is there any Churchillian leader on the scene today?

Phenomenomics 101

In the same way that military strategists cannot explain Israel's military successes, Israel's economic performance would seem to exceed its resources. Because in truth, and in fairness, Israel has plenty of problems holding it back. Among its biggest problems is a burden of regulation that, although it has protective value against the destabilizing influence of big business seen in the U.S., also stifles entrepreneurship.

This difficulty, which is real, in some sense highlights the extraordinary upside potential in Israel's economy. Remove the shackles of administrative barriers to success, prudently, of course, and the world will come to see Israel's true economic power unleashed far beyond its current start-up phase.

In this, as in the small country's remarkable military victories, the output of Israel's economy seems to defy its diminutive size miraculously. The Bible explains the nature of this kind of surprising economic performance in a short narrative (II Kings 4:1-7) in which an impoverished widow appeals to the prophet Elisha for help when a creditor threatens to enslave her two children.

Elisha inquires after the widow's remaining possessions. Her answer: nothing other than a single flask of oil. One might ask: Why did Elisha need this information? If God was going to perform a miracle for her anyway, couldn't He just have Elisha write her a big check, or cause her to find a hidden treasure chest somewhere?

But in the way that is characteristic of all God's miracles recorded in the Bible, as previously discussed, Divine assistance occurs by what appears to be natural means. The woman had oil - so that was to be the source of her salvation.

Elisha tells the widow to borrow as many vessels as she and her children can possibly find, then "close the door" and pour. The Bible never wastes words. Why was that seemingly unneeded instruction about the door included? The medieval commentator Rashi explains that performing the economic miracle in secret provides it respect.

So too with the Start-Up Nation. Even a largely antisemitic world is in awe of Israel's economic miracle. Israelis must also scrounge for vessels – be they impoverished new immigrants, a culture of risk-taking and a love of learning – and apply all their creative strengths to see those jugs filled.

At the conclusion of this miracle, when the widow finds no more vessels, the text says "and the oil stopped" (literally, "stood up"), which Rashi explains to mean that the price of oil went up. Concealed miracles – market demand or other favorable conditions – combined with effort and excellence similarly provide respect for Israel's economic achievements.

Not only were the widow and her sons able to repay their creditors but they had enough to live on for the rest of their lives. "You and your children will live with the remainder," are the story's final words.

Anti-Israel Boycott, Divestment and Sanctions (BDS) activists notwithstanding, there will surely always be a market for Israeli ingenuity. Take Jimmy Carter, a one-term president remembered mostly for his passivity and inefficacy while 52 U.S. citizens were held hostage in Tehran for 444 days; the former president has gained greater notoriety as an *ex*-president involved in a number of left-wing causes, particularly anti-Israel activism[20].

Yet Carter's love of life exceeds his hatred for Israel. Four months after the ex-president revealed in August 2015 that he was diagnosed with Stage 4 melanoma, a serious and usually fatal form of cancer, it was revealed that a new alternative cancer therapy has successfully inhibited the malignant cells from proliferating.[21] Despite the role of Israeli medical scientists in researching and testing the drug, Carter has not announced any plans to stop taking it.

As surely as West Point analysts find that Israel's military performance exceeds its observable capabilities, so too will the Jewish state's future prosperity likely continue to surpass the expectations of economists and even ex-presidents.

CHAPTER FIVE
Eternal Values

Giving up your bus seat for an elderly person is a good deed, more noted perhaps in the breach than the observance. An Alzheimer's Society survey in Britain showed just 2 in 5 adult respondents said they made this small sacrifice.[22] Lamentably, the world over, it is not uncommon to see young, healthy people seated while the old and weary stand nearby.

In this context, it is interesting to note the simple three-word priority-seating injunction found on Israeli public transportation: *mipnei sayvah takum* – "You shall rise before the elderly." This author has not found any international studies showing how Israelis and non-Israelis stack up on this particular practice, but it's worth mentioning that the sign is not based on any inelegant verbiage of a bus-company bureaucrat but rather a direct quote from the Hebrew Bible – one of the 613 *mitzvot*, or commandments, that Jews are religiously obligated to perform.

Ceding one's bus seat to an elderly person is but one

practical application of this *mitzvah*. From a religious point of view, a Jew should rise out of respect if an elderly person merely enters his presence, even in an empty room.

The general point is that conditions in Israel are uniquely nurturing, not only of the country's brave soldiers or its high-quality and abundant produce, but also of Jewish values.

Chances are high that even your average "secular" Israeli who goes out to dinner is eating kosher food, in a restaurant serving either meat or dairy according to Jewish dietary law requiring their separation[23] – while his diaspora counterparts, often even those who regularly attend synagogues, routinely eat in non-kosher restaurants.

Take a look at the Knesset. Its hallways and its parliamentary floor, are covered with men wearing kippot, and with some female parliamentarians or staffers wearing traditional head coverings. About a third of its members today are religious – an exponential increase unimaginable even a decade ago. The same trend – an entirely new one – is seen throughout government. Israel's new national police chief, Roni Alsheich, its Shin Bet (Israel's FBI) director Yoram Cohen and its Mossad (Israel's CIA) chief Yossi Cohen are bearers of Jewish tradition.

Israeli society is undergoing a process of re-Judaization, a gradual reversal of the de-Judaization that intensified at the end of the Jewish people's long exile. Influenced by Europe's enlightenment and other Western secular trends, Jews shed their religious traditions to such an extent that Judaism actually became anathema to many of Israel's founders. These radical secularists often went out of their way to discourage religious practice, a stance with particularly destructive effects on Jews who immigrated from Middle Eastern countries. These immigrants were raised traditionally, but felt the dislocating effects of entering a society that viewed religious mores as primitive.

Nevertheless, gradually but forcefully Israel is experiencing a religious reawakening. A plausible explanation may derive from the unceasing war, terror and hatred confronting Israel. As the American aphorism puts it, "there are no atheists in foxholes," meaning that the unique vulnerability felt by soldiers, who know they may not return home from battle, makes them spiritually more sensitive and more aware of their dependence on a Higher Power for their very survival.

Ofer Winter, when he was commander of the elite Givati Brigade (Israel's Marine Corps equivalent and not a specifically religious military unit), tapped into this feeling in a letter to his troops prior to a dangerous battle in Israel's 2014 war in Gaza, in which he offered the prayer:

"I lift my eyes heavenward and call out with you: 'Hear, O Israel: the Lord our God, the Lord is One.' O Lord, God of Israel, make our path successful as we are about to fight for the sake of your people Israel against an enemy who blasphemes your Name."[24]

This, and many similar openly religious statements by Winter, provoked much gnashing of teeth amongst Israel's shrinking secular elite at universities and in the media, but was well received among soldiers who are regularly seen visiting Israel's Western Wall for spiritual strength in seemingly greater numbers and increasing frequency.

As distinct from Israel's Haredi religious sector whose moves toward army service are progressing but slowly, members of its national religious (*dati-leumi*) sector not only wholeheartedly embrace military service but have come to dominate its officer corps, much as kibbutzniks once did in the state's early years.

These Orthodox officers now represent at least a quarter of new officer cadets, a tenfold rise from the level found in the early 1990s.[25] The motivation of these young men is infectious and influential. In the 2006 war in Lebanon, Major Roi Klein, an elite paratrooper in Israel's Golani Brigade, jumped on a live grenade, saying the Shema Yisrael prayer as he died to save his men.

Except for a few cranks at dying institutions like *Haaretz* (Israel's oldest but least read major newspaper), which questioned his serving as a role model[26] for living in a supposedly illegal outpost in Samaria, Klein's name is known and honored nationwide as a true hero of Israel.

The waning anti-Zionist minority – and in fairness even a portion of patriotic secular Israelis – are animated by the worry that a rise in the number of Torah-observant Jews will risk the introduction of religious coercion in the army, which is widely seen as the most inclusive and fundamental Israeli institution.

Generally speaking, religious soldiers' prime concept is one of *keruv*, which means drawing their secular brethren closer to their traditions warmly and lovingly.

Any actions that might lower esteem for Jewish observance is to be strongly avoided. Mutual respect amongst religious and non-religious soldiers is the on-the-ground reality in the IDF.

(In truth, there is no current shortage of religiously coercive types, not so much in army life but in other pockets of Israeli society; from the standpoint of Jewish law. These are responsible for actions that have the effect of distancing their fellow Jews from their heritage and are considered a grievous transgression.)

While religious-secular friction unfortunately still rears its ugly head from time to time, the key trend is that Israeli Jews want more Judaism.

The last major survey of the Israeli Jewish public's beliefs, observances and values showed a marked shift toward tradition – a notable swing in what has been one of the world's most secular populations. It would seem that that 2009 study[27] is already significantly out of date and likely *understates* Jewish religious sentiment; in other words, one should expect a further acceleration in Israel's Jewishness in the next national survey.

Perhaps it comes back to that 'no-atheists-in-foxholes' explanation. When terrorists spring knives on unsuspecting Israeli citizens - as has been occurring in the fall and winter of 2015,2016 on an almost daily basis - and the world's reaction is muted or even exculpatory[28], but deafening when such terror strikes another country such as France; the notion that Israel is a nation that dwells apart and has a unique destiny starts to sink deeper into Israeli consciousness.

At the man-on-the-street level, Israelis have clearly become more nationalistic. That is tantamount to saying more religious, since the Jewish faith is based on nationality and on the Jewish nation's unique relationship with God, in contrast to other religions that are, above all, sets of beliefs.

It takes very limited conversation before a Jewish cab driver, not wearing a kippah, expresses his pride in Israel, the army or says "Baruch Hashem" ("Thank God"), an expression formerly associated with just religious Jews that is today heard everywhere by everyone.

Singing God's Praise

Perhaps the most telling expression of changing Israeli cultural norms can be heard in the country's popular music. While Western-style vacuous lyrics are far from unknown, popular songs from rock to rap abound in references to God and appeals for His blessing and help.

Take Rami Kleinstein, a major Israeli pop star. His debut album in 1986 achieved gold status, but his 1997 album "Everything You Want" (*Kol Mah She'tirtzi*) propelled him to the triple-platinum level. Its romantic lyrics about his wife (this in itself marks a distinction from the generally non-marital context of Western pop lyrics) are written poetically: "Your hair scented with intoxicating coconut, a skilled pencil paints the lips..."

The same Rami Kleinstein in 2014 sings of a different aroma and ambience in his hit "Small Gifts" ("*Matanot Katanot*"):

"Another Friday...the table is set, childhood pictures

on the wall; convoys of white [Sabbath attire] returning from the synagogue; and the fragrance that scratches my heart; to a small treasure, that old song; that has been passed down to us through the generations."

The song continues until it culminates in the Kiddush, the blessing Jews make at the start of their Sabbath dinners every Friday night for millennia. In live appearances, the non-kippah-wearing pop star walks into a swooning crowd of fans who join him in singing: "For You have chosen us and sanctified us. Blessed are You God Who has sanctified the Sabbath." (He touchingly covers his bare head when singing the portion of the song containing this prayer.)

Consider also Gad Elbaz, a popular singer from the religious camp, who hit the charts in 2013 with the catchy tune "God is King" ("*Hashem Melech*") whose constantly repeated main lyrics are: "God is King; God was King; God will be King forever and ever."

Something is clearly going on at the street level when songs like these (and there are many, many others) top the pop charts. When all the Jewish people honor the same King, it sublimates their deepest yearnings in a spiritual direction while having the effect of creating a deep sense of unity.

And it's not just the songs expressing a return to Judaism, but of course their singers. It has been reported that Kleinstein now refuses to perform on the Sabbath and Jewish holidays, and regularly puts on phylacteries, a Torah mitzvah incumbent on men.[29] The same can be said with increasing frequency about a raft of celebrated film stars and musicians, soldiers and novelists.

Uri Zohar, perhaps the most celebrated comedian, actor and director in the previous generation, is today a rabbi, and two of his sons married two of the (newly religious) daughters of Israel's most famous singer Arik Einstein. The ever expanding list of returnees to tradition is long and frequently updated.

"Who Bore Me These?"

In considering the increasing proportions of returnees to tradition, one should not neglect to weigh the enormous multiplier effect of Jewish demographic expansion. Having children is the ultimate expression of confidence in the future, and in this realm, the Jewish state truly dwells apart from *all* other economically advanced nations, whose population growth rates are in decline.

According to the CIA World Factbook 2015 estimates, U.S. fertility – with one of the higher rates amongst advanced economy Western nations – is below the crucial population replacement level of 2.1, registering just 1.87, a number that could not be achieved without substantial immigration flows. In contrast, Israel's fertility rate according to the CIA is a robust 2.68, though other sources such as the World Bank and Population Reference Bureau give significantly higher figures, at 3 and 3.3 respectively.

In a TV interview with Israel's Channel 2,[30] Guy Bechor, a professor of Middle Eastern Studies at Israeli university IDC Herzliya, puts the population trends in perspective, noting "an awesome ascent" in the Jewish population rate (accentuated by a "crisis" in the falling birth rate among Palestinian Arabs).

Citing 2013 figures from a variety of sources, Dr. Bechor says the average native-born Israeli family (the majority of whom are non-religious) are having 3.4 children on average. This rate is accelerating so quickly that he calls "4 [children] the new 3." Meanwhile, national-religious families are having 5 children on average, while Jewish residents of Judea and Samaria (who are over-whelmingly religious) are having 6 children on average. In contrast, their American Jewish cousins are having just 1.25 children on average.

Interestingly, he cites data showing California as having the lowest birth rate in the U.S. of just 1 child per family and says the reason given by demographers is "self-fulfillment," meaning that affluent Americans seeking "the good life" want to be freed from the restrictions of raising children. But, he adds, ask Israelis why they are having more children and they give exactly the same reason: self-fulfillment.

"Only one country has the chutzpah to have a rising birthrate," he says. Of course, continued Jewish immigration further strengthens Israel socially, economically and militarily – as does the simultaneous steady decline in Palestinian births (down from 5 births per woman in 2003 to 2.7 in 2013) and net emigration (of 10,000 to 17,000 a year) primarily to Europe.

(It should be noted that demographics as they relate to Israel and the Palestinians is an inherently controversial topic, and there are competing sets of numbers that paint an even opposite story – for those willing to lend credence to numbers coming from the Palestinian Central Bureau of Statistics.)

The prophet Isaiah (49:18-21) comments on Israel's future demographic shift, portraying a sudden, unexpected turnabout in Jewish population trends – perhaps foretelling what Dr. Bechor called "an awesome ascent."

"Lift your eyes around and see; all of them have gathered, have come to you….from your ruins and your desolate places and destroyed land

Now you will be crowded by inhabitants, and those who would swallow you will be far away.

The children of whom you were bereaved will say in your ear, 'The place is too narrow for me, move over so I can dwell.'

And you will say in your heart, 'Who bore me these, as I was bereaved and lonely and exiled and rejected. And these – who raised them?

I was left alone by myself.

Where are these from?'"

CHAPTER SIX
Infernal Values

"I'm empty and aching and I don't know why."
– from the song "America," Paul Simon,
Simon & Garfunkel, 1968

America's military is strong, but dangerously misdirected; its economy - an attractive house of cards as an ill wind slowly brews; but its culture has already collapsed with the only question: how much farther it can fall.

Canon City, Colorado is a town nobody would ever have heard of. In the depths of what sophisticated urbanites refer to snobbishly as "flyover country," the town does not even qualify as a suburb of the much larger Colorado Springs, 45 miles away, whose reputation for heartland wholesomeness has earned it the nicknames "the evangelical Vatican" and "the Christian Mecca."

Yet Canon City's claim to infamy arose in November 2015 when it was found that high school students in the town of just 16,000 people were circulating sexually explicit photos of at least 100 different teens through their cell phones, a practice termed "sexting."

When sexting has reached Canon City, it has surely penetrated all of America.

Americans take enormous pride in their neighborhood schools. They generally buy their homes only after first carefully vetting the local schools according to the values they identify with most. The more affluent typically look at how well the school prepares its students for college. Across the socioeconomic spectrum, enormous weight is placed on sports teams, usually football, baseball or basketball, though upper-middle-class families flatter themselves with the sort of games found in New England prep schools – archery, rowing, lacrosse and so forth.

But little, if any, thought is given to the reality that they're sending their innocent children to promiscuity training camps.

A 2012 study published in the medical journal *Pediatrics*, probably already out of date and understating the problem, shows that 20% of *middle-school* students report receiving child pornography text messages.[31] At the high school level, the studies report a majority of the kids now have engaged in what was once referred to as marital relations before they graduate.[32] By the time they get to college, they're met by a plethora of well-funded programs with counselors who normalize, promote and celebrate sexual activity divorced from any emotional or spiritual meaning, and without any serious understanding of the consequences in terms of self-respect, sexually transmitted diseases, abortion or the inability to bear children in the future (because of STDs or delayed marriage).

America, and its culturally similar European cousins, are steeped in licentiousness. Its culture is designed to train girls to fulfill male sexual fantasies. Women called by the title "feminists" – ironically, because they want to adopt masculine sexual characteristics – are primary indoctrinators in this ideology.

These are deliberately obtuse people – the radical professionals among them, that is – who have covered millions of pages of "Women's Studies" books and papers in pretzel-like logic meant to deny the most obvious of truths: that women and men are fundamentally different.

But the untruths of these millions of pages are refuted by the tens of billions of dollars spent annually on sexual entertainment: women may be the "stars" but the consumers are almost all men. After the first male-nudity pornographic magazine targeting "sexually liberated females" entered the market, its editors eventually admitted that its "readers" too were men.

These facts about pornography are equally true for the tens of billions of dollars spent annually on prostitution. Subtracting prostitution and pornography from the GDP would likely send many an economy into deep recession; South Korea, Spain, Russia and maybe a couple of the Scandinavian countries might need IMF loans to tide them over.

But rather than encourage men to adopt inherently

female attitudes toward sexuality, which emphasize privacy, modesty and family, and which have long formed the foundation of civilization, Western society does just the opposite. The results include depression, eating disorders and even suicide.

Dr. Miriam Grossman, a former psychiatrist at UCLA, wrote a book ("Unprotected," 2007) documenting the severe emotional harm she witnessed among college students, especially females, navigating the college campus "hook-up" culture that failed to provide them stability and clarity about relationships. Revealingly, she felt she had to publish the book anonymously because of its unorthodox views; before investigators discovered her identity.The book's author was "Dr. Anonymous."

Evidently, in the America of today, critiquing behaviors with traumatic emotional outcomes could ruin a person's professional reputation.

Indeed, parents who would rage against their children if they dared to smoke a cigarette feel mute (if they even notice anymore) regarding America's toxic, sex-addled society. U.S. culture – its TV and movies particularly – trains its citizenry from the earliest ages that parents are out-of-touch oafs lacking the moral authority to inculcate values. To critique sexual behavior is seen as old-fashioned, repressive and hypocritical – as if parents and their children are on an equal footing when it comes to intimate relationships.

While Hollywood and Madison Avenue are high on the list of antagonists, parents are the most to blame. No one would ever think of taking an open sewer pipe and pump its filth into their living rooms, but the fancy large-screen TVs found in most households are the parent-enabled conduit pouring unwholesome ideas and images directly into their children's minds on a daily basis.

Entertainment is hardly the only way American society coarsens its youth. Divorce, now afflicting nearly half of all marriages, deprives children of stability and often thrusts emotionally scarred children in the direction of unwholesome non-parental influences (though there are severe cases where dissolution is the lesser evil).

According to a World Health Organization report, "the region with the world's largest illicit drug market is North America" It further characterizes the use of these drugs as "largely a youth phenomenon."[33] America's youth – "empty and aching", to quote Simon and Garfunkel's 1960s song "America" – find all sorts of ways to fill the spiritual void. According to the U.S. Centers for Disease Control and Prevention's most recent biannual survey, about a third of America's high school youth currently consume alcohol, and about a quarter are current marijuana users.[34] The latter figure will likely only increase given the sudden and surging tide of public opinion in the direction of legalization or decriminalization of marijuana in recent years; only in a minority of U.S. states is the psychoactive drug still prohibited.

Another mark of societal deterioration that probably goes mostly unnoticed because of its utter ubiquity is vulgar language. Whereas a generation ago, children who used such language would quickly hush up when teachers or other adults approached, today it is common to hear children unashamedly use such language loudly, in public, and in front of their parents. Perhaps that is how their parents speak in their homes.

This author has observed an ugly trend over years of business travel. At large conferences catering to a business audience, one hears vulgar language not just in casual conversations over food and drinks, but from the speaker's podium – in front of mixed crowds of thousands, and not just occasionally but at every single conference!

Whereas once it was considered indecorous for men to use such language in the presence of ladies, today unsalutary words just fly out of the mouths of CEOs and other publicly prominent people, men and women alike. Perhaps they feel that such references lend an aura of frankness to their discourse without realizing that it merely attaches to themselves the indignity of the private activities to which they are alluding.

And apropos of private affairs, go to an ATM machine to take out $20 in June, and you are likely to be commanded by your bank to celebrate Lesbian, Gay, Bisexual and Transsexual Pride Month. Another previously rare phenomenon that is rapidly gaining acceptance is "gender transition," where the highest authority in the land, the president, was quick to weigh in, establishing with much fanfare the White House's first gender-neutral bathroom.[35] The administration has also added sex-reassignment as a covered Medicare benefit, and has contributed a legal brief in a federal circuit court case in support of a transgender male high school student's demand to use the bathroom of his choice.[36]

In the past, no banker ever felt it was his job to honor male-female marital relationships – but such is the scope of the governmental and corporate imposition of alternative relationship models on Americans both willing and unwilling. The pace of change has been dramatic.

In 1996, fearful that the Constitution's "full faith and credit clause" requiring the states to honor the laws of other states, would legitimize a ruling by Hawaii's Supreme Court permitting gay marriage, the U.S. Congress passed the Defense of Marriage Act, formalizing the traditional definition of marriage as between a man and a woman. A wave of state legislatures followed suit. But then the judicial branches of state after state struck down many of these laws until finally, in 2015, the Supreme Court of the United States invalidated laws that voters passed democratically in the individual states.

Regardless of the legal arguments pro or con, the court's decision aligns well with the rapid acceptance of non-traditional marriage in the U.S. A Gallup survey tracking Americans' views on the moral acceptability of certain controversial issues shows that views have evolved in a permissive direction on *all* issues, and that the biggest change has occurred in approval of homosexual relationships, which 63% of the public accept today, compared to 40% in 2001.[37]

Today, a solid majority of Americans back having a baby outside of marriage (61%); "doctor-assisted suicide," i.e., allowing physicians to kill their patients (56%); and gambling (67%). That last one should not surprise since nearly every state government sanctions and indeed actively promotes gambling through official lotteries; the citizens' lost wages and diminished character are a big business for revenue-hungry states.

Also lost in these profound social shifts has been respect for freedom of conscience. Take for example Brendan Eich's job as CEO of web browser Mozilla Firefox. In 2008, Eich joined the majority of California voters in supporting a California ballot proposition defining marriage as between a man and a woman. He also donated $1,000, as a private citizen, to the initiative's organizers.

Six years later, in April 2014, gay activists initiated a social media campaign against Eich, demanding he step down from the company he founded. In a craven and spineless announcement of his departure, the company's chairwoman Mitchell Baker hailed the importance of equality and free speech, but then shoved the latter out the window, together with Eich, in a model for contemporary corporate political correctness.

"We have employees with a wide diversity of views. Our culture of openness extends to encouraging staff and community to share their beliefs and opinions in public," Baker ironically wrote in the company's blog.[38]

Though giving into a lynch mob, she added another layer of self-congratulatory deceit in painting Firefox as an exemplar of free speech:

"While painful, the events of the last week show exactly why we need the Web. Now all of us can engage freely in the tough conversations we need to make the world better."

Thus, support for traditional moral concepts is something that Americans must hush up about if they know what's good for them. Not only will the government and courts come down on them, but even being the founder and CEO of your company (and even the inventor of JavaScript, as Eich was) is not reason enough to let you keep your job if you're known to support traditional marriage.

In an age of political correctness, it is possible that some may misconstrue disapproval of proscribed relationships as attacks on the dignity of individuals exhibiting such behaviors. It's worth stating emphatically that every person has inherent worth and should not be reduced to any one behavior, least of all an objectionable one.

Shredding the Foundations of American Society

The rate at which America banishes traditional morality and weakens freedom of conscience is probably roughly in proportion to the number of Americans who pass through college campuses, especially the elite ones. Much has already been written on political correctness on college campuses; when one thinks it couldn't get any worse, these avant-garde institutions manage to plumb new depths of degeneracy.

The latest trend involves what's called "trigger warnings," where emotionally fragile college students protest that their exposure to some idea – often a literary classic that contains non-PC ideas – will cause emotional distress. Even high schools are getting in on the game, banning, or placing trigger warnings before books such as "The Adventures of Huckleberry Finn."[39] Mark Twain's anti-slavery novel, which has generally been regarded as the greatest literary classic in American literature, now supposedly gives students the vapors because of its use of the N-word, which is liberally deployed in at least every other sentence in the hip-hop music they listen to daily.

Recently, an anti-PC activist, as a gag, pretended that the distribution of copies of the U.S. Constitution at Vassar College "triggered" her.

"They were handing it out and as soon as I saw it, you know, I started to not be able to breathe, hyperventilating. My vision went blurry and I just – kind of just lost control," she said in the secretly videotaped encounter. After the campus equal opportunity official validates her feelings, the reporter posing as a student suggests putting the Constitution through a paper shredder, to which the administrator responds with alacrity: "Yes, I think we have a shredder in the front office there. Did you want to do it with me?"

The two even discuss the idea of banning the Constitution from campus, though the college administrator gently suggests it might be needed in the campus library "for research purposes."

The video shows a similarly sympathetic reaction to the same gag at Oberlin College.[40]

U.S. college campuses have succeeded in shredding, literally and figuratively, the foundations of American society – its values and its Constitutional legitimacy. For all of its historic glory, its freedom, tolerance, natural beauty and other exceptional qualities, contemporary American society is not a place decent people can raise or educate their children without taking extensive precautions.

CHAPTER SEVEN

America's Next Crisis: The Loaded Gun Waiting to Go Off

Jihad is a holy struggle, a legitimate tenet of Islam, meant to purify oneself or one's community."

Which Muslim leader offered this definition? Was it Islamic State's Abu Bakr al-Baghdadi? Of course not. That naïve statement came from John Brennan, the current director of the CIA.[41] Brennan was deputy national security advisor for homeland security when he made those remarks in a 2010 public speech, demonstrating just how far political correctness enables one to rise in government these days.

The problem is a bipartisan one. No less than President George W. Bush – not even a week after the deadliest terrorist attack in U.S. history – rushed to declare that "Islam is peace."[42] Bush doubtless had good intentions; he was seemingly trying to prevent any freelance violence on the part of angry Americans. But had the religiously oriented president looked into his own Bible, assuming he knew where to look (this is not meant to be offensive; Biblical literacy today is extremely low), he might have seen the description of Ishmael and his descendants in Genesis 16:12:

"And he will be a wild ass of a man, his hand against everyone and everyone's hand against him, and on top of all his brothers he will dwell."

The religion of Mohammed, from its inception, has spread through the sword, so Bush's kindly evaluation was divorced from historical reality (which matches the Biblical description).

Islamic State's al-Baghdadi captured the spirit of Islam more accurately when he said:

"O soldiers of the Islamic State... erupt volcanoes of jihad everywhere. Light the earth with fire against all dictators."[43]

The banal reassurances of Western leaders, just like the soothing statements of Islamic leaders to Western audiences, are the least valuable way to learn about Islam. The Western world, including the United States, lacks any practical understanding of the civilization most opposed to it.

Yesterday, the enemy was al-Qaeda, a group no one had heard of on September 10, 2001; today Islamic State joins a long roster of hostile groups bearing Arabic names and Muslim themes. Even if the U.S. eliminated every member of each of those groups, a new group no one has presently heard of would rise to resume the battle against Western civilization.

Many jihadists are already present in the U.S. and new members are infiltrating the U.S. through the re-settlement of refugees of Syria's civil war. In recent years the U.S. has adopted policies that restrict the ability of authorities to filter out immigrants with hostile intentions. For example, FBI guidelines established in 2012 assert that "religious expression, protest activity, and the espousing of political or ideological beliefs are constitutionally protected activities that must not be equated with terrorism or criminality absent other indicia of such offenses" [44]

So, if a refugee from Aleppo attended a politically active mosque whose members turned out on the streets for Hezbollah, or the al-Nusra Front, immigration officials are supposed to view him as though he had merely been training to become an exemplary American, exercising his future constitutional rights.

If you think this is hyperbole, note the recent revelation by Lt. Gen. Michael Flynn, until recently the head of the U.S. Defense Intelligence Agency. Flynn told a German newspaper that U.S. forces had arrested ISIS terror chief al-Baghdadi in 2004 before determining him to be "harmless" and letting him go.

The problem, apparently, was that, unlike al Qaeda leader Osama bin Laden, he had not been seen brandishing a gun. Rather, Flynn said:

"Al-Baghdadi in contrast spoke in a large mosque in Mosul, on the balcony, almost like the Pope. He appeared in a black robe, as a holy scholar and declared the Islamic Caliphate."[45]

In other words, he would have contributed to America's religious diversity, strengthening the Constitution. The red carpet, or at least an Islamic prayer rug, would have been rolled out for him had he only applied for U.S. citizenship.

A country that cannot accurately define its enemies is in serious trouble.

Indeed, numerous official statements over recent years yield the conclusion that Washington sees the weather as today's gravest danger.

"I am convinced that no challenge poses a greater threat to our future and future generations than a changing climate," President Obama said in August 2015 in the same paragraph in which he listed what, to his mind, were the lesser threats: the wars in Iraq and Afghanistan and the "devastating recession."[46]

In an earlier speech to a military academy graduating class, the president announced that fighting global warming would be a new priority, and even offered a novel environmental analysis of the current conflict raging in Syria, focusing not on that country's brutal regime or competing terror factions, but rather on the following:

"It's now believed that drought and crop failures and high food prices helped fuel the early unrest in Syria, which descended into civil war in the heart of the Middle East."[47]

Britain's lugubrious Prince Charles, a longtime member of the Church of Sustainability, has added his voice to this thesis, telling Sky News:

"Some of us were saying 20 something years ago that

if we didn't tackle these issues, you would see ever greater conflict over scarce resources and ever greater difficulties over drought, and the accumulating effect of climate change which means that people have to move. And in fact there's very good evidence indeed that one of the major reasons for this horror in Syria, funnily enough, was a drought that lasted for about five or six years."[48]

"Funnily enough," when Prince Charles' country and its French allies divided up the Middle East between themselves not 20 but 100 years ago, they paid no heed to the sociological integrity of the ethnic and religious groups contained within these artificial borders.

Syria's Arabs, Kurds, Turkmen, Armenians, Muslims, Christians, Alawites, Druze, Shia and Sunni groups are not as similar to each other as Iowans are to Minnesotans. To paraphrase the Prince, in fact there's very good evidence that most Syrians have reacted in horror to the minority Alawite regime's heavy reliance on state-of-the-art torture chambers to force the majority's submission.

Thinking people should be wary – for at least another generation – of accepting the claims of "climate scientists." A deep religious belief in global warming led defenders of the faith at the University of East Anglia's Climactic Research Unit to falsify key data in a 2009 scandal that came to be known as Climategate. A more recent report published in London's *Telegraph* newspaper avers that tampering with the temperature remains a favorite pastime of "climate scientists," infecting key data sources such as NASA's Goddard Institute for Space Studies in the process.[49]

With American soldiers' guns trained on the sun while terrorists infiltrate America's borders; with an economy kept alive on a unique form of steroids that make the richest Americans richer while doing precious little to ameliorate problems in the real economy faced by a middle class that has seen its financial standing deteriorate; with an ever-devolving culture that disperses unintelligence to elite segments of society, who then foist their toxic values on an unwitting population, where exactly is America headed?

All the World's a Stage

In *As You Like It*, Shakespeare immortalized the concept of history as drama in the now common expression "all the world's a stage." But it was the great Russian playwright Anton Chekhov who explained the theory behind it.

"If there's a rifle hanging on the wall in Chapter 1, it absolutely must go off in Chapter 2 or 3," he said.

On the stage of history, there is presently a heavily loaded gun pointed at the United States.

With the state of America's foreign policy, its economic mismanagement, its permissive social atmosphere and, it should be added, the still unhealed wounds from a history of slavery, racial discrimination and harmful social, cultural and educational policies, that gun looks ready to detonate.

Following Chekhov's gun theory, it would seem that the two biggest pieces of artillery presently facing the U.S. are the nuclear weapons that U.S. administrations of both parties allowed the North Koreans and Iranians to develop.

While American presidents, secretaries of state and national security advisors invested their energies in unachieved and unachievable Arab-Israeli "peace" processes, or climate conferences and the like, these two adversaries with unambiguous records of malintent were allowed to get away with building a murderous arsenal meant for the United States and its European allies.

In the modern era, Western political leaders value, above all, negotiated agreements and pomp-filled signing ceremonies. They lack any appreciation for the worthlessness of their adversaries' signatures - and these days are prepared to dispense with the signature part anyway, as seen in Chapter 3.

After decades of painstaking negotiations (and expensive bribes, such as two light-water nuclear reactors the U.S. was building for Pyongyang as inducement to forgo the building of facilities that could be used for non-peaceful purposes), the North Koreans in 2006 tested the nuclear weapons they had developed under cover of negotiations with both the Clinton and Bush administrations.

Pyongyang is currently developing an intercontinental ballistic missile (ICBM) that could make the celebrated lifestyle of the U.S. West Coast a thing of the past. With unsurpassed naïveté, the U.S. actually agreed to take the issue of ICBMs off the table in its nuclear talks with the ostensibly green-energy seeking Iranians. This, despite the fact that the purpose of ICBMs is, as the name implies, to reach distant continents – i.e. North America.

Israel's Prime Minister Binyamin Netanyahu repeatedly tried to warn the Obama administration about the Iranian missile threat. For this he was treated by Obama as an escaped leper on his March 2015 visit to Washington, where he told the U.S. Congress:

"…ISIS is armed with butcher knives, captured weapons and YouTube, whereas Iran could soon be armed with intercontinental ballistic missiles and nuclear bombs. We must always remember – I'll say it one more time – the greatest dangers facing our world is the marriage of militant Islam with nuclear weapons. To defeat ISIS and let Iran get nuclear weapons would be to win the battle, but lose the war. We can't let that happen."[50]

U.S. Enemies Don't Have to Shoot Straight to Create Chaos

What those who doubt the capabilities of these foes might not know is that U.S.-style technical precision is no longer a requirement for military effectiveness. In a little known, but gravely serious development, America's enemies need only manage to shoot a dirty nuclear bomb anywhere into the U.S. atmosphere. The electromagnetic pulses (EMP) thus emitted would incapacitate the electric systems, computers, smart phones and other devices on which modern life depend.

Congress established an EMP Commission in 2008 to understand and prepare for these risks, but the commission's warnings have gone largely unheeded.

In fact, the very next year, newly elected President

Barack Obama pushed Congress hard to spend $787 billion on political pork as a response to the economic crisis. Those funds could have been used to build back-up power grids to secure vital infrastructure in the face of an attack – funds that would have had the additional merit of putting people to work across the country while addressing a genuine need. (The 2009 "stimulus" package was severely criticized at the time for the paucity of jobs it created – i.e., for its lack of economic stimulation.)

Also relatively unknown, in April 2013, a team of terrorist snipers snuck into a Silicon Valley power station and very professionally knocked out 17 electrical transformers, costing utility company PG&E $15 million in damage. The attack was sudden and would seem to be a calculated terrorist attack meant to probe the extent and effects of power outages and the resources of U.S. utility companies.

Though the experts who penetrated the plant escaped undetected, the FBI in February 2014 concluded that the incursion was not an act of terrorism.[51] As if to refute – or embarrass – the FBI, the very same facility was breached a second time in August 2014, even though the plant's security had been upgraded since the previous attack.[52] The government seems to view the affair as the act of vandals, but independent experts see the military-style incursions as training for future attacks that could cause cascading blackouts nationwide.

Awash in Debt

Whatever the "black swan," or unforeseen triggering event, will be, the U.S. economy is unlikely to be able to withstand the blow, as discussed in Chapter 4. American elites have grown so fragile that the business cycle has been effectively banned. Stocks and bonds seemingly are only permitted to go up, as they have for the past six years, supported by zero-rate easy money. Meanwhile, Americans are heavily indebted and most are unprepared for the economic consequences of losing their jobs. With what currency, and with what credibility, will the U.S. government – which extended or pledged $24 trillion to bail out the economy in the previous crisis – rescue the country in the coming crisis?

Even the smartest policymakers lack the ability to prevent economies from correcting for excesses permanently. Moreover, as discussed, the problems that contributed to the previous crisis have not been ameliorated and indeed have been aggravated in many respects. For example, systemically important financial institutions that were seen as "too big to fail" in 2007 are even bigger today. The U.S. and other leading economies are more leveraged today than in 2007; a 2015 McKinsey Global Institute study found that global debt has increased by $57 billion since that time, increasing the advanced-economy debt-to-GDP ratio by a further 17 percentage points.[53]

Visitors to the United States from poor countries are typically awed by the eye-popping affluence they see. Americans who travel abroad return home with a renewed appreciation of the wealth and comfort they possess. But far less understood is that so much of the Western world's wealth is based on *borrowed* money; still less understood is what would happen to that wealth if

the bankers (Japanese and Chinese households prominent among them) called those loans.

Since the previous crisis, almost every advanced *and*
developing country – nearly every single one covered by
the McKinsey study – has increased its leverage, thus
making them that much more vulnerable to the next financial shock. Ireland's debt-to-GDP ratio increased by
172 percentage points since 2007, giving the country a
debt ratio of 390%. Thus it would take Ireland nearly four
years' worth of the country's entire national income to
pay off a year's worth of its total debt.

Interestingly, Israel has been alone among advanced[54] countries in *reducing* its debt leverage by 22 percentage points during this period (to 178%, compared to
a debt-to-GDP ratio of 233% for the U.S.).

Desperate Times, Desperate Measures

History suggests that government authorities and
central banks will do their utmost to maintain economic
confidence, and they will succeed – until some unexpected event triggers a panic for which none of their reassurances make any difference.

The government will need money to respond to
the crisis, but it will be hard-pressed to come up with
the needed funds, since at precisely the time the world
should have been *deleveraging* (since excessive debt was
understood to be a key cause of the previous crisis), it has
been *re-leveraging*.

As discussed in Chapter 4, the Federal Reserve can
only lower today's near-zero interest rates to the extent

that people are attracted to the idea of accepting 80 or 90 cents for each dollar they agree to lend to government. (Some European central banks have recently driven rates into negative territory without scaring away savers. But it would seem to be a dubious proposition over the still untested long-term when customers' mattresses pay better rates.)

Additionally, the U.S. government is already running a huge budget deficit and can expect to see tax revenues plummet in response to a new economic crisis.

China, as discussed, is no longer the banker of last resort; it's got its own problems, and Japanese leverage exceeds even Ireland's, as discussed above.

In this extreme environment, it is conceivable that governments will seize wealth from the segment of the population that has extra money. These days, after much international coordination regarding banking transparency, governments have a good grasp of who has how much money and where it can be found. The days of stashing money in a Swiss or Virgin Islands based bank account, with the idea that nobody knows about it, are long gone.

More restrained governments in the next crisis may simply issue new tax demands, or worse, "borrow" the money, with a pledge to pay it back at some future time. The more desperate ones may just take the money by executive fiat overnight, reporting the news to your local newspaper the next day.

If this sounds far-fetched, consider a recent precedent. When the tiny island nation of Cyprus fell into excessive debt, its more affluent citizens awoke the next morning to find out that the government had raided their bank accounts.[55] And if you think, "Well, that's Cyprus – where is Cyprus?" – know that it was the mighty European Union that imposed this draconian solution, taking as much as 100% of savings from those with deposits over 100,000 euros.

Another possibility might be a more populist raid on wealthy corporations. Exxon-Mobil's corporate execs could awake one morning to find out that Uncle Sam is the new CEO, after a suitable pretext is found.

Something like this too has already happened. In 2012, Argentina took over the country's largest energy firm, YPF.[56] Of course, Buenos Aires paid for the shares – with a gun to YPF's head, that is. The expropriation took place a short time after YPF had discovered a major oil field. The Latin American giant later awarded Chevron – a YPF competitor – the right to develop that field.[57]

A more extreme option would be outright repudiation of debt, but that complicates future economic cooperation with the cheated parties; the least extreme option would be increased general taxation of the population. But that could be a dud at a time of falling economic production, whereas a quick confiscation would seem capable of generating substantial assets when they are most needed.

Call to Arms

Besides a sudden wealth tax, another seemingly plausible scenario in the next economic crisis would be a full-scale military mobilization. If the crisis' trigger was a military event, then such a response would be logical. America may find itself confronting war, even on its mainland.

But there is also an economic logic. During the Great Depression, one out of four Americans was out of work. That unemployment rate did not return to single digits until Americans mobilized for World War II.

The government, even if run by liberals cautious about the use of military power, might see other advantages in a draft. In the midst of the previous economic crisis, President Obama's chief of staff Rahm Emanuel was noted for saying: "You never want a serious crisis to go to waste."[58] The military is a strict command and control environment. A cynical government may wish to avail itself of this captive audience of young Americans in areas unrelated to the war effort.

The U.S. is overdue for a crisis. Wars and economic depressions are reliably recurring facts of history. Even if precipitated by an external event, internal moral and social decay typically paves the way as people let down their guard during the "good times." In the next chapter, we will see what might be done in light of America's current vulnerability.

CHAPTER EIGHT
How to Save a Sinking Ship

Americans get a chance to choose a new president every four years, but the problems heretofore described are beyond the office of the presidency to correct.

Even were the next president a person of exemplary character and Churchillian leadership skills – and all that would certainly help and is much to be hoped for – it must be understood that the roots of these problems lie in American society even if it is American elites who have served as the yeast activating the nation's toxic brew of social, moral, economic and political ills.

What's more, even an upstanding president would have to face the reality that America is currently politically dysfunctional. The two main parties automatically align at polar extremes on every issue and seem to genuinely hate each other. In this sense too, the U.S., which used to be admired for its political moderation, has joined Europe.

The 20th century French writer Andre Maurois, to whom this kind of fractious governance was intimately familiar, once remarked:

"The heads of our political parties may be compared to rival officers in charge of a large ship. As a passenger on that ship, I can allow them, at most, to hate one another, but under no circumstances will I consent to their hatred causing the ship to sink."[59]

That is the position in which Americans now find themselves. It's a difficult position because politicians mirror, even if in exaggerated form, the views of their constituents. Thus, Americans need to undertake the hard work of fixing themselves. It's a values leak that is sinking the U.S.S. America. The encouraging news is that individuals need not feel helpless because their own actions, individually and collectively, can achieve the needed rehabilitation.

America's Historical Values Betrayed

America's moral dissolution is not merely lamentable in itself, but it is foremost a betrayal of the very values that made America great.

Franklin Delano Roosevelt gave voice to this once more widely understood idea when he said:

"We cannot read the history of our rise and development as a Nation, without reckoning with the place the Bible has occupied in shaping the advances of the Republic .... where we have been truest and most consistent in obeying its precepts, we have attained the greatest measure of contentment and prosperity."[60]

Before British colonials settled the U.S., no one would have had reason to forecast America's future greatness. Its economy was primitive, its land containing tremendous natural resources but presented formidable barriers to their exploitation. The principal advantage America had was not that its founders were British (and thus were heir to more liberal political and economic institutions) but that they were British *dissenters*. They fled Britain to protect their moral ideals. The Pilgrims knew and took the Bible seriously and were purveyors of philosemitism in a world that had and has mainly demonstrated vicious antisemitism.

The Pilgrims and their Puritan descendants in colonial America tried to live specifically by "Old Testament" ideals – in other words, by the values of the Hebrew Bible. Furthermore, their progeny, the Founding Fathers, learned the Bible, and very often the Hebrew language, in university, which in those days – perhaps for the first and last time in history – embraced moral values.

America's second president, John Adams, well represented early America's take on Judaism and the Hebrew Bible in a letter he wrote to a friend:

"I will insist the Hebrews have [contributed] more to civilize men than any other nation. If I was an atheist and believed in blind eternal fate, I should still believe that fate had ordained the Jews to be the most essential instrument for civilizing the nations... They are the most glorious nation that ever inhabited this Earth. The Romans and their empire were but a bubble in comparison to the Jews. They have given religion to three-quarters of the globe and have influenced the affairs of mankind more and more happily than any other nation, ancient or modern."[61]

Ken Spiro, Abraham Katsh, Paul Johnson and Eric Nelson are among the contemporary scholars who have shown how America's most precious institutions – its freedom, its Constitution, its separation of powers – derive from Jewish Biblical ideals.

And, indeed, the Hebrew Bible itself offers God's promise that "I will bless those who bless you [the Jewish people] and those who curse you I will curse and through you all the families of the earth will be blessed." (Gen. 21:3). That blessing was given to Abraham, but it is repeated to Isaac (and not to his half-brother Ishmael, progenitor of Islamic civilization) and to Jacob (and not to his brother Esau, regarded in Jewish tradition as the progenitor of Western civilization).

Indeed, this blessing is immediately demonstrated in the generations of the patriarchs: the Hittites regarded Abraham, the Hebrew foreigner in their midst, as a "prince of God;" Isaac brought tremendous economic development to the Philistines, though they foolishly envied his greater wealth; Laban, Jacob's crooked Aramean father-in-law, acknowledged many times that it was Jacob who made him rich.

Furthermore, in the Jewish people's first exile to Egypt, we see early on the explanation for Egypt's rise to greatness when the Hebrew slave Joseph first takes up residence in the house of Potiphar: "And it was from the time he [Potiphar] appointed him [Joseph] over his house and over all that he had, God blessed the house of the Egyptian because of Joseph and it was that the blessing of God was on all that he had in the house and in the field."

The later books of the Bible, such as the Book of Ezra and the Second Book of Chronicles, reflect how pro-Jewish policies coincided with Persia's rise to greatness. Recorded history picks up the same theme and tracks many examples of how countries like England, Spain, Napoleonic France – or modern-day Europe – rose or fell in relationship to their policies toward Jews.

The medieval ruler Boleslaw III shrewdly invited the Jews fleeing the First Crusades to Poland as a means of developing the Polish economy, and other leaders throughout history have acted similarly and benefited thereby.

But no country ever showed greater solicitude to the Jewish people – granting them full and equal rights and religious tolerance from its very inception – than the United States. America's historically unique economic might and political and military strength – and spectacular rise out of an undeveloped wilderness – would seem to confirm the explanatory power of this Biblical theory of history.

In modern history, President Harry Truman recognized the newborn State of Israel in 1948 over the objections of U.S. Secretary of State George Marshall, who thought America's national interests lay with the more numerous and oil-rich Arab states. Richard Nixon cut through layers of bureaucratic red tape, as only a president could do, to get vital military supplies to Israel amidst the existential danger of the 1973 Yom Kippur War.

But the U.S. relationship with Israel has gradually evolved, in a negative direction, over recent decades. While the hostility and repugnance Israel evokes in Barack Obama has been vividly displayed for seven straight years of his presidency, it is interesting to consider – in light of the blessings and curses theory of history – that the worst economic crisis affecting the U.S. since the Great Depression occurred in the final year of the presidency of George W. Bush, who was generally thought to be a pro-Israel president.

Indeed, Bush's warmth toward the Jewish state seemed quite genuine, but, as always, one must look at concrete actions more than words or feelings. In the latter days of Bush's presidency, he all but turned over his foreign policy to his secretary of state, Condoleeza Rice.

Rice has plenty of company in the long list of abysmal U.S. diplomats – there have been worse before and since – but her stewardship of U.S. foreign policy marked the first full flowering of the wrong turn America took after the Cold War ended.

Through the decades long prism of U.S.-Soviet rivalry, it was possible to view the U.S. as taking Israel's side while the Russians backed Israel's enemies; thus, there were the good guys and the bad guys. But once the U.S. became the sole superpower, America's foreign policy elites started assuming more of an "honest broker" role.

Rice in particular should have better understood the

perils of neutrality between the two sides, having been a Soviet Union expert at Stanford. Patriotic Americans such as Rice generally took umbrage at arguments, common on U.S. college campuses, that morally equated the U.S. and the U.S.S.R. America should have backed its "client" Israel to the hilt and declared another Cold War victory; in so doing, it would have only strengthened its own standing in the region and gained respect as a true world power.

Yet U.S. diplomats since the fall of the Soviet Union have made a "neutral" peace process a primary focus, relentlessly pushing Israel to make rash territorial concessions while accepting ambiguous verbal assurances from Palestinian negotiators who typically take back their soothing words in English when addressing Arabic-speaking audiences the next day.

The Clinton Administration ushered in an era of relentless war, terror and bloodshed with its Oslo "peace" process that continues to this day as a result of the two gun-toting terror fiefdoms in Gaza, Judea and Samaria (the latter two commonly referred to as "the West Bank"). Before the ink had dried on the Oslo Accords signed on the White House lawn in September 1993, arch terrorist and Noble Peace Prize winner Yasser Arafat had this to say at a mosque in Johannesburg, South Africa in May 1993:

"The jihad will continue. . . You have to come and fight a jihad to liberate Jerusalem. . . No, it is not their capital. It is our capital."[62]

But by November 2007, Rice was recklessly ready to

bypass the decades of failed trial periods of peaceful Palestinian autonomy and cut straight to a Palestinian state. Adding insult to injury, Rice defamed the Jewish state in a closed diplomatic session in Annapolis, Maryland, in which she was reported to have compared her experience growing up as a black girl in the segregated South to that of Palestinians in Israel:

"I know what it's like to hear that you can't use a certain road, or pass through a checkpoint because you are a Palestinian. I know what it is like to feel discriminated against and powerless."[63]

Of course, Rice's slander got it completely backwards. Checkpoints and security precautions in Israel are meant to prevent Palestinians from terrorizing the Jewish population. It's the Jewish shops, restaurants, malls and community centers that require security guards. Willing customers can march right into any Palestinian commercial center they want – Arab merchants are unconcerned about the possibility of Jews detonating themselves. If only blacks in the Jim Crow South had security guards working on their behalf to prevent KKK terrorists from brutalizing black schoolchildren!

Seven years later, in 2014, Obama Administration secretary of state John Kerry took a page out of Rice's distorted history book warning that Israel risked becoming an "apartheid state" if it did not, in effect, speedily accept U.S. proposals for a Palestinian terror state in its midst.[64]

With Friends Like These, Who Needs Enemies?

Without laboring through the minutiae of U.S. Middle East diplomacy, the key point is that the U.S. made a very poor transition from an anti-Soviet superpower to the world's sole hyperpower. Administrations of both parties have displayed a lack of clarity about U.S. interests, irresolution and a strange deference to European foreign policy preferences (such as the establishment of "Palestine").

From the point of view of Israel's geopolitical situation, U.S. foreign policy has become more of a menace than its many Arab enemies. Israel's political and military elites would never acknowledge this and possibly would not even agree with it. Growing up in a world where Israel has been isolated, they have valued the generally warm ties and military support from America.

It must be said: Israel has demonstrated its ability to repel any combination of its Middle Eastern enemies, yet could be fatally weakened by establishing a terror state within its slim boundaries - as the U.S. demands with ever increasing insistence. Worse, U.S. statesmen from administrations of both U.S. political parties demand, and with increasing shrillness, that Israel desist from doing the one thing that would do the most to strengthen its security in the region: increasing Jewish settlement of Judea and Samaria.

Thus U.S. diplomatic aggression (under the guise of its new honest broker role) - specifically the full frontal assault represented by its current Palestinian statehood obsession - seems sufficiently hostile to trigger the economic crisis, or curse, described in the Book of Genesis.

(Note that the word "blessing" in Hebrew has a specifically economic connotation more than the spiritual nuance assumed in English; thus a financial crisis is precisely the type of curse one would expect from cursing Israel.)

The world's financial commentariat, struggling to figure out the failure of the economic "recovery" that Barack Obama has promised but not delivered, have dissected his fiscal decisions in vain. The problem lies more in Obama's foreign policy than his economic policy.

Every time Hamas launches a rocket targeting Israeli civilians, ensconcing the rocket launchers amidst their own civilians, the *predictable* result includes a) a surgical Israeli military response that should merit a Nobel Peace Prize for the lengths to which efforts are made to limit civilian damage; and b) shrill denunciations from the White House and State Department (and of course the UN and other foreign offices) about "disproportionate" Israeli responses that are deemed "not helpful." The *unpredicted* result may be a further erosion of U.S. and Western economic strength.

(Note: The U.S. is not alone in the world. Russia under Vladimir Putin has shrewdly shifted the country's foreign affairs in a decidedly pro-Israel direction. It is interesting to observe that despite its enormous political and economic challenges, Russian power has steadily strengthened over the past decade.)

A More Rooted America

So there you have it: America is plagued by internal moral dissolution – of the kind that distances America from God, as we saw in the ideal discussed in Chapter 1: "And your camp shall be holy"; and externally, America's foreign policy elite has adopted a posture of contempt toward Israel, engendering a promised Biblical curse.

Yet a single solution can address this dirty duo at one and the same time: America needs to return to its roots.

A mere two weeks into the summer of 2014 war in which Israel was responding to Hamas attacks against Israeli civilians through its network of terror tunnels, President Obama personally telephoned Prime Minister Benjamin Netanyahu to demand an immediate cease-fire[65] – which would allow the terrorists to regroup and inflict more terror on Israel.

An America returned to its roots would do the opposite. If a Judeophilic John Adams were still president, he would rush over the Marines to assist in rooting out Hamas, much as his successor Thomas Jefferson did against Arab terrorists "on the shores of Tripoli" during the Barbary Coast Wars. George Washington, Benjamin Franklin, Alexander Hamilton, John Jay and James Madison would all be charter members of AIPAC. Their moral outlook would demand it no less than their calculated assessment of U.S. national interests.

In a more rooted America, the words of Thomas Jefferson recording his conversation with the ambassador from Tripoli (prior to the Barbary Coast Wars) read as if the ink has not yet dried from the page:

"It was written in their Koran, that all nations which had not acknowledged the Prophet were sinners, whom it was the right and duty of the faithful to plunder and enslave; and that every mussulman who was slain in this warfare was sure to go to paradise. He said, also, that the man who was the first to board a vessel had one slave over and above his share, and that when they sprang to the deck of an enemy's ship, every sailor held a dagger in each hand and a third in his mouth; which usually struck such terror into the foe that they cried out for quarter at once."[66]

Nowadays, the likes of James Baker, Madeleine Albright, Colin Powell and Hillary Clinton – in addition to previously mentioned presidents and secretaries of state – insist that Israel succumb to terror. Is it any wonder then that they fecklessly fight their own terror wars?

A year after he commanded Israel to lay off Hamas, Obama defended his Syria strategy against charges of inadequacy following a terrorist attack on Paris:

"No, we haven't underestimated our abilities. This is precisely why we're in Iraq as we speak, and why we're operating in Syria as we speak. And it's precisely why we have mobilized 65 countries to go after ISIL, and why I hosted at the United Nations an entire discussion of counterterrorism strategies."[67]

As mentioned in Chapter 2, beginning with the first Iraq war, the U.S. took to forming international coalitions in its military escapades, but one could be forgiven for viewing the participation of Albania in its current 65-member anti-Syria coalition as signifying more of an evasion of responsibility than an invasion bearing credibility.

While the U.S. limply battles ISIS, Russia has now become seen as the main foreign power in Syria. Obama's remark about having "hosted at the United Nations an entire discussion" well sums up the shrinkage of American power today.

America Needs a Good Rabbi

America is badly demoralized and badly needs to be remoralized. In early American history, lapses in the founding population's religious faith was followed by religious revivals that historians have termed "The Great Awakening." These episodic bursts of spirituality during the 18th and 19th centuries did much good, including providing the impetus for the movement to abolish slavery and promote women's rights. Notwithstanding a less broad spiritual awakening in the 20th century (leaving out coastal America), the past century should perhaps be viewed by future historians as The Great Slumber.

As discussed in Chapter 6, the decline in moral values has grown severe. Sexual looseness is especially problematic since, like Pandora's box, it is hard to contain once inhibitions have weakened. A reaction against the sexual revolution was once expressed through a 1980s-era group called the "Moral Majority." Under today's circumstances, would anyone dare use a name like this in modern America?

What is needed today is the formation of a Moral Minority that in time can expand to encompass a remoralized majority. But the model is not the former Moral Majority, whose appeal was generally limited to Southern, evangelical Christians. Nor is it the 10 Command-

ments, which a recent survey showed were mostly un-
familiar to a majority of Americans who, with much
greater ease recalled the ingredients in a Big Mac and the
members of TV's "Brady Bunch" family.[68]

Rather, it seems timely to pull out from the mists of
time another list that has become the world's best kept secret, less known than the special sauce McDonald's uses
on its signature burger and easier to remember than the
10 Commandments: to wit, the Seven Commandments
of the Children of Noah.

According to Jewish tradition, the revelation at Mt.
Sinai included moral instruction in two forms: a written
Torah to be sure, but also an oral Torah that was passed
down from teacher to disciple over the generations.

When Christianity appropriated the Hebrew Bible
as its main religious text, the Oral Torah was not yet written down. Under extreme religious persecution, the rabbis eventually wrote down the Oral Torah – the Mishna,
and its explanation, compiled by later authorities, called
the Gemara (together, the Talmud).

What this essentially means is that non-Jews have
the Cliffs Notes on this ancient body of law, whereas Jews
have much deeper sources from which to draw, including Talmudic discussion of the Seven Commandments
of the Children of Noah.

As the name implies, these laws are considered bind-
ing on all of humanity: God did not desire a relationship
with Jews alone, but with all His creations.

Jewish tradition records that at an early stage of humanity – that is, after the common ancestor of all man-

kind, Noah, survived the Flood – God laid down seven ground rules for all of humanity going forward.

These rules ban idolatry; illicit relationships (e.g., incest, adultery, homosexuality, bestiality); **murder;** theft; blasphemy; eating the limb off a living **animal; and** require a system of courts and laws to enforce the previous six.

Simple as they seem, these laws can be explored endlessly in a fashion similar to the way Jews re-read the Torah each year, ever extracting fresh insights. They can also be understood as broad categories rather than singular precepts; for example, theft can be carried out brazenly and publicly (i.e., robbery), covertly (i.e., burglary), even mentally (i.e., through creating a false impression), and Jewish law details these numerous prohibitions. Similarly, notions about the prevention of cruelty to animals and respect for God's creations form part of the teaching related to not eating a limb off a living creature.

It is interesting that ancient legal systems such as the Code of Hammurabi, which predates the Mosaic code, include many of the Noahide laws. For example, the ancient world, closer to memories of the flood, understood the requirement against illicit relationships in contrast to today's Western world which increasingly embraces them.

But how are the nations of the world to learn these laws – that is, to really learn them, as opposed to merely reading them?

Before the revelation at Sinai, the Torah presents God as saying: "You will be for me a kingdom of priests and a holy nation" (Exodus 19:6).

Priests are leaders and Torah teachers. This is really what is meant by Jews being the "chosen people." The Torah's plan seemingly is that there be one group that can model for the rest of the nations demonstrating what it is like to live in relationship with God.

Because the Jews have been hounded across the whole earth throughout history, they've never really been afforded that opportunity, and many have forgotten what they were supposed to be teaching. Perhaps now is the time for both Jews and non-Jews to work together on this remoralization project.

The more Americans, and other nations as well, become reacquainted with their moral obligations and the Bible generally, based on technically correct interpretations from knowledgeable Jews who remain bearers of the Sinaitic tradition, the less keen they will be to support politicians working to create a terrorist haven alongside the Jewish state.

Indeed, appreciating that such moves would spawn terror and economic chaos in their own midst, they would be more likely to struggle to achieve the reestablishment of Jewish sovereignty over the whole of the Land of Israel in active pursuit of blessing rather than curses.

CHAPTER NINE

Assuming the Mantle of Superpower

The social and moral pathologies afflicting the West are present, in greater or lesser measures, in Israel as well. The country's modern-day founders were secular Europeans, and the country's laws, institutions and culture were influenced by and have kept pace with trends in the West.

But as described in Chapter 5, Israel's traditional ways are sprouting above this European topsoil to reveal the nation's true Jewish essence.

For example, Chapter 6 described how the U.S. has gone so far as to effectively repeal one of the Seven Commandments of the Children of Noah through a 2015 U.S. Supreme Court decision affirming gay marriage. Israeli law does not allow for this possibility since all family law matters are under the jurisdiction of the country's chief rabbinate, which permits marriage or divorce according to the dictates of Jewish law.

Nevertheless, a segment of the Israeli population prefers alternative lifestyles. Indeed, like other Western nations, Israel too is home to gay pride parades. But, more than in the West, these events also attract huge and passionate counterdemonstrations.

Heinously, one Jew went so far as to violently attack some of the gay marchers in 2005, and again in 2015 – just weeks after his release from prison for the first attack. The second time this deranged murderer took a life; under Torah law his life too should be taken.

But more characteristically and more peacefully, religious Jewish leaders organized a "modesty parade" on more than one occasion as a response to the gay pride parade.

The concept is significant, as Jewish tradition views intimate relationships as inherently demanding of privacy. Highlighting sexuality in public goes against the grain of tradition; what's more, the word "pride" also rubs the wrong way in that Jewish tradition demands humility and views pride as one of two characteristics that righteous people must always shun (anger being the other).

Israel today assuredly abounds in immodesty; it's just that nowhere else are there obstreperously vocal counterexamples. And when murderers are kept locked up in prison (or, preferably, given the death penalty), such voices will likely find a receptive audience. It is not uncommon to hear people who are *not* from the religious sectors of society express strong disapproval of gay pride parades in Jerusalem (if not Tel Aviv), referring to the city's inherent sanctity; indeed, the Knesset has occasionally taken up measures to ban such parades from Jerusalem specifically given the currency of such feelings.

Additionally, Israel's truly unique demographic surge has spawned large families, the key building blocks of what are called "family values." Thus, the market exists for a rethinking of Western permissiveness.

Israel's Turnaround

As previously discussed, wars, terror and a world unable to judge Israel fairly have done much to remind Israel's Jews that they are a nation dwelling apart (Exodus 19:6).

No Israeli Jew wants these wars, of course, but they're having the effect of turning the Jewish people toward the only Ally on Whom they can rely. For a long time, many Israelis had hoped that the United States would be that ally. America is the most powerful and prestigious country, and Americans have stood out in supporting Israel. But as we have seen, its governing class and permanent bureaucracy have undermined this special relationship, just as they have allowed the threat of terrorism to the U.S. itself to gain powerful momentum.

Yet the upside of an utterly friendless world is that it cultivates military figures like Col. Ofer Winter (discussed in Chapter 5). When there's no one else to turn to, soldiers like Winter cast their gaze heavenward.

A more recent budding of this Jewish spirit was seen in the maiden speech of Israel's current deputy foreign minister Tzipi Hotovely. (Prime Minister Binyamin Netanyahu kept the foreign minister role for himself, so Hotovely is in effect the official most involved in running the ministry's day-to-day affairs.)

Hotovely told the assembled Israeli diplomats in the May 2015 address that they need to begin bringing in the Bible as a source for Jewish rights to the land. The appeal apparently raised eyebrows among a diplomatic corps more accustomed to citing international treaties and UN and League of Nation charters as sources of Israel's international legitimacy.

But Hotovely was right. The best arguments in the world, and the best Jewish lawyers presenting them, have failed to persuade an unpersuadable world of the justice of the Jewish presence in the Land of Israel.

Hotovely thus wisely cited the very first comment by the foremost commentator on the Bible – Rashi, who anticipated this phenomenon of unreason.

To paraphrase, Rashi asks: Why does the Bible begin with the creation of the world? If the Torah is a catalogue of commandments to the Jewish people, shouldn't it begin with the first of those commandments? Rashi answers (in the name of Rabbi Yitzchak, possibly his own father) that the nations of the world will contest Jewish claims to the Holy Land. Consequently, the beginning of Genesis shows that God is the Creator of the world and can therefore dispose of its land as He wishes. He gave Canaan to the Canaanites but then determined they were morally unfit and gave that land instead to the Jewish people.

Rashi's argument may not carry any weight with the State Department, which would immediately demand clarification if Israel's U.S. ambassador made it. But it is ultimately the best argument Israel has and one which its own population needs to hear asserted.

What Israel Needs to Do

The full flowering of the Jewish state has already achieved lift-off and will doubtless proceed apace, with or without the support of Israel's government. Nevertheless, the government can speed things along.

To that end, the most urgent priority would be to fight Israel's social problems with *greater* severity and determination than it fights Hamas. Israel's police and volunteer organizations should work together to stamp out an illegal sex trade by fighting the suppliers – the Russian mob is thought to be the biggest player – as well as the demand side. The Knesset should enact severe penalties including long sentences with hard labor, and Israel should make innovative use of shaming techniques, publicizing the names and faces of customers.

The police should similarly treat drug traffickers with severity, and employ aggressive education and treatment for users, drawing especially on religious organizations who might help address the spiritual void that addicts seek to fill through chemical stimulation.

The model nation can demonstrate that it is possible and necessary to achieve total victory. The Talmudic sage Raish Lakish said: "One who comes to purify himself, [Heaven] assists him."

And as the Maccabees showed in their war against the Greeks that is memorialized in the festival of Chanukah, when the enemy fights you spiritually (as the hedonistic Hellenists did in their war against Torah), you fight back physically.

And when they fight you physically, as the Persians did – promising to annihilate every single Jew as commemorated in the holiday of Purim – you fight back spiritually, through prayer and national unity.

Whether the enemy du jour is Hamas, Hezbollah, the Palestinian Authority or state actors like Iran; Israel needs to adopt a policy of total victory over the enemy. In the 2014 war against Hamas and its terror tunnels, the Jewish state's most powerful weapon was a spiritual tool – as befits this type of war – namely, the unprecedented national unity that followed the horrific kidnapping of three Jewish boys: Eyal Yifrach, Gilad Shaer and Naftali Fraenkel, may God avenge their blood.

For 18 agonizing days in June 2014, the IDF turned the country upside down searching for the boys. Israelis and Jews worldwide prayed for the redemption of their captive brethren and felt a profound, shared sorrow when they were found dead. Hundreds of thousands of Israelis attended their funerals and then participated in the week of intense mourning which Jewish tradition dictates following the burial of a close relative.

This national unity buoyed the IDF's efforts, led bravely by men such as Col. Winter, in the war against Hamas, sparked by the kidnapping but sustained by the terrorists' horrific network of tunnels, some of them under Israeli playgrounds and schoolyards near the Gaza Strip.

While Israeli unity and the IDF's military excellence are sufficient to defeat their enemies, a highly correctable

diplomatic problem hamstrings Israel's ability to pros-
ecute its military needs: its relationship with other nations, but most especially with the United States.

As discussed in the previous chapter, U.S. President
Barack Obama waited just two weeks (during which he
offered his sympathy for Israel's plight) before demanding that Israel lose its war with Hamas by holding its fire.

There are many other ways in which the U.S. and
its Western allies severely harm Israel's national interests.
For one thing, the U.S. under Obama has taken to funding Hamas, when the terrorist group joined forces with
the "moderate" Fatah-faction (founded by arch-terrorist
Yasser Arafat) that rules the Palestinian Authority. Yet
the PA engages in daily incitement to terror in contravention of its Oslo-initiated treaty obligations.

Obama's actions, implicating U.S. taxpayers in funding terror tunnels, terrorist incitement and financial aid
to the families of terrorists, only build on the actions of
the Bush administration which initiated "security assistance" to the PA.

Most Americans are probably unaware of the fact
that U.S. military personnel are training Palestinian Authority "police" and the State Department is providing
this terrorist kleptocracy with hundreds of millions of
dollars a year. Given Chekhov's literary theory requiring
a rifle in Chapter 1 to go off by Chapter 3, the presence
of U.S. military advisors on the side of the Palestinians
implies that U.S. armed forces will one day be put to poor
use if this is not soon called off.

For all these reasons – U.S. restraints on the IDF and

U.S. funding and training of Palestinians – Israel's most urgent foreign policy priority must be to cease accepting any U.S. foreign or defense aid. The reason is obvious. Israel feels beholden to the United States because it receives this strings-attached financial grant.

But as discussed in Chapter 4, the Israeli economy has grown. It no longer needs foreign assistance, and the government probably mostly desires the funds as testimony to the world, and even more to itself, that Israel has friends.

On the stage of history, the Palestinians are a club used by the Muslim and Christian worlds as a prop to beat up the Jews. They have no other function. They have no economy. They export only terror. They subsist on the largesse of international donors, foremost the European Union, but increasingly the United States as well. On a per capita basis, the Palestinians have received more than 15 times the amount provided to Europeans through the Marshall Plan.[69] The Europeans rebuilt their war-torn continent whereas Palestinian leaders have built terror tunnels, funded wars and stashed away billions of dollars for themselves while their people live in misery.[70]

The U.N. also offers aid, and while that international institution sponsors an organization that assists the world's refugees, it also hosts UNRWA, a superfluous organization devoted uniquely to Palestinian refugees. That group has not decreased over time but expanded tenfold, while no other refugee population in history has remained in camps for generations after their initial displacement. That is because the Arab countries refused to resettle Arab refugees fleeing Israel after the 1948 war, and the world has expressed its desire to continue its war against the Jewish people through them, their descendants and their cousins still living in Israel. UNRWA and other U.N. organizations, including "peacekeepers," have frequently actively intervened on the side of terrorists in violation of their mandate.

Fortunately, just like Col. Winter and Deputy Foreign Minister Hotovely, rising Israeli leaders such as Moshe Feiglin, Naftali Bennett and numerous others, are increasingly vocal about ceasing to accept U.S. aid. Israel's economic growth trajectory will add back the missing revenue very quickly, presently equal to just 1% of GDP, while the Jewish state gets an immediate payoff in terms of its diplomatic and military maneuverability.

The Disappearance of American Jews

While there's much more Israel's government can do besides cracking down on crime and asserting its foreign and defense policy independence, most of the change will continue to come from the grass roots of Israeli society.

As discussed in Chapter 5, Israel is in the process of re-moralizing. Until recently, one of its most popular TV shows, called "Srugim" (knitted yarmulkes), followed the personal lives of religious Jewish characters. Srugim's success spawned a new show called "Shtisel," this time set in a Haredi, ultra-Orthodox setting. Imagine if Ozzie and Harriet returned as America's top TV show, only rather than cute, comedic gags involving the wholesome 1950s family, the show focused on its characters' religious yearnings – on how their relationship with God impacted their human relationships.

Such a spiritual awakening is not presently occurring in the U.S.; rather, as discussed in Chapter 6, a harsh dulling of the conscience is taking place, and since America's urban centers are the manufacturers of these cultural trends, city dwelling American Jews are first in the firing line.

It's not merely that American Jews are having just 1.25 children per family – a rate lower than the American average of 1.87 and a sure path to physical extinction – but such children as they do have are increasingly not Jewish. Under Jewish law, only the child of a Jewish mother is considered Jewish, and the intermarriage rate today is now beyond demographic repair.

The last major survey of American Jews by the Pew Research Center in 2013 found that a majority, 58%, intermarry.[71] The trend is persistently ruthless, as the intermarriage rate was 43% in 1990 and 17% in 1970.

But the 58% figure masks the true dilution, since 10% of American Jews surveyed were Orthodox; since they by definition (discounting for survey reporting problems) adhere to Jewish law, they skew the numbers. Subtract the Orthodox and the intermarried population rises to 71%. Among those describing themselves as secular, the intermarriage rate was 79%.

Furthermore, since these trends are not static but rather have kept moving in the same direction, it seems all but certain that the next Pew survey will reveal an intermarriage rate for non-religiously observant American Jews in the 80-percentile range or higher. This represents a demographic "game over." American Jews, despite or perhaps because of their manifold contributions to American society, turned out to be more American than Jewish.

A 2014 follow-up Pew survey of religion across America was no more encouraging.[72] Indeed, Jews more than any other religious groups in America were "empty and aching" without knowing why. Majorities of Muslims, Catholics, Buddhists and Protestants (in that order) report thinking about the meaning and purpose of life, while only a minority of Jews (45%) do so.

Perhaps most tragic of all – apart from (and in explanation of) the majority who eat non-kosher food and support same-sex marriage – is that just 11% of U.S. Jews (a proportion matching the Orthodox Jewish sector) believe in the Divine authorship of the Torah. That is, the American branch of the people who introduced the Torah and its Godly message to the world no longer believe in it; they are truly messengers who forgot their message.

The minority of American Jews who are religiously observant will increasingly find themselves making uncomfortable choices, such as whether to attend a relative's bar or bat mitzvah ceremony that has little to do with any mitzvahs. Indeed, among the broader U.S. Jewish population, these events have become shallow coming-of-age style parties, like a Sweet Sixteen ceremony, only replete with violations of Jewish law (such as candle-lighting ceremonies – a direct contravention of the Torah prohibition against kindling a flame on the Sabbath). In recent times, there has been a plague of viral videos showing bar mitzvah boys amidst Vegas-style scantily clad dancers, speeches denouncing belief in God, or dances with effigies of Barack Obama, today's version of the Golden Calf.

Come Home

In a game-over Jewish America, those living a life rich with meaning and the empty and aching alike have much to gain in making Israel their home.

The boys of the Netzach Yehuda battalion described in the first chapter are cases in point. At very young ages, these kids have already experienced the esteem-enhancing experience of having made the world a better place.

Take Netanel Silverman, a Brooklyn native who signed up for 14 months of service in Netzach but voluntarily extended his service to 41 months, ending in 2015. The now 25-year-old and his comrades apprehended numerous Hamas terrorists, including some involved in planning attacks, others in funding them, and others who carried them out. Netanel knows his way around a dark alley and how to protect vulnerable Jewish communities adjacent to hostile population centers. This valuable experience informs his current training in nursing school.

In a wide-ranging discussion with the author, the words that Netanel seemed to repeat the most were "caring," "family," and "*mesirut nefesh*" – a Hebrew term meaning self-sacrifice.

The first staff sergeant described how army commanders "are always there with you" – they're not sitting in an office away from the field of battle, as is common elsewhere. A general, he says, is not too high in rank to carry an injured civilian on a stretcher – if he happens to be on the scene at the time. He cites the example of Jerusalem mayor Nir Barkat, who – not once, but twice, and with his own hands – foiled a terrorist attack when he happened to drive by as a young Arab was stabbing a Jew; 11 years earlier to the day, Barkat ran headlong toward a bus that a terrorist had blown up and saved the life of a girl who was rapidly losing blood by staunching the wound.[73]

It's this "*mesirut nefesh*" that Netanel observes everywhere.

"When I first started out here [in 2011], I would go Friday night to the Kotel [Jerusalem's Western Wall]. There could be anywhere between 50 and 200 people any given night but no one goes away hungry. Someone would always come to us to invite us for a meal.

"Everywhere you go there's someone taking care of you; you can rely on the fact that someone will give you a ride," a common practice in Israel where car ownership is less universal than in the U.S.

He also observes that there's a Jewish rhythm to life in Israel, in that everyone's preparing for the Sabbath or holidays at the same time. "Go to the bank and they're giving out jelly doughnuts," the food Israeli Jews customarily eat during Chanukah, as their American counterparts eat latkes. He also praises the extraordinary geographic diversity – "drive a half-hour in one direction and you've got deserts, a half-hour in another direction and you've got forests."

As a rare American in his battalion, Netanel was touched when Rabbi Bar-Chaim requested his mother's phone number, and surprised when he spoke with his mother a few days later and found out Rabbi Bar-Chaim had already called her to report on his welfare.

The first staff sergeant said that whenever a rabbi visited his base – a minimum of three times a week – everything would stop as the boys gathered around to learn and to be inspired. Further, rabbis' visits to isolated lookouts where soldiers were lonely and cold, provided tremendous moral support. But the most appreciated encounters of all were the visits that came before the start of the Sabbath or holidays. "It's the times when everybody wants to be with their family that means the most."

While rabbis served *in loco parentis*, fellow soldiers were his brothers in arms, and Israelis he didn't know supplied meals, rides and other needs, Netanel, who came to Israel as a lone soldier in 2011, soon found his world populated by even closer family.

In the summer of 2013, his older brother and his wife and children made Aliyah; in the summer of 2014 his sister and her family moved to Israel; in the summer of 2015, his mother came. "They came in stages; it was not planned," he says. In due course, he hopes his other siblings in New York will make the move.

What Defines a Superpower?

And that's the thing of it. Israel is not a nation like any other. It is one big extended *family*. And Judaism is not a religion like any other; it's a *relationship* between God and each Jew, and with the Jewish people.

And despite the problems swirling around the

world, and around Israel particularly, no nation other than Israel has the capacity to build bridges of peace between peoples. The Jewish tradition of laws understands Islam; its ethical teachings encompass Christianity.

Slowly but surely, gradually but with certainty, the Jewish people who a generation ago were left for dead in the pits of hell that were Europe's concentration camps, are coming back to life, as a people, as a family. As the prophet Ezekiel envisioned in the Valley of Dry Bones, their sinews are being laid upon them, their skin is covering them up, their breath is coming into them, their bones are coming together.

"I will put my spirit into you and you will live; and I will place you upon your land. And you will know that I God have spoken and done it – the word of God." (Ezekiel 37:14)

This re-Judaization process is well under way. Even lost tribes, Jews from places like Ethiopia and Nepal, or forced converts whose descendants live in places like Portugal and Peru, are coming back home. European Jews tired of the antisemitism of France or Ukraine are returning.

Jews in the United States may be the slowest Jewish population in the world to make the move, no doubt mainly because of the comfortable lifestyle and peaceable relations with non-Jews. Increasingly, though, one observes that American Jews are reluctant to identify with Israel because they have absorbed the anti-Israel messages conveyed by U.S. media and universities. In an environment that has grown so toxic that UCLA's Student Council spent 40 minutes in February 2014 debating whether they could let student Rachel Beyda serve on the advisory body because she was Jewish and therefore presumed morally compromised, many Jewish students are in no hurry to identify with the most hated country in the world.[74]

Yet these demoralized Diaspora youth could experience what feels like an alternative universe were they to come to Jerusalem on the holiday of Sukkot (Tabernacles) during the annual "International Jerusalem March." In a preview of Zechariah's prophecy that in the Messianic era the nations of the world will bring their offerings to Israel's eternal capital, thousands of marchers from dozens of countries around the world offer astonished Jerusalemites smiles, songs, gifts and unending expressions of love – mostly in English. The marchers come from every corner of the earth – Angola, Brazil, China, Finland, South Korea, you name it.

In contrast to the frequent waves of terror, the love bombs these mainly Christian pilgrims hurl are balm for the wounds of discouragement that are the lot of the Jewish people in a still hostile world. One day of this exhausting cascade of love can make up for more than a few governmental press conferences yet again denouncing Israel.

With all of America's greatness, and its lure to immigrants across the globe, the attraction people feel is highly self-interested. They want prosperity, they want freedom.

But love transcends selfishness. Non-Jews who love

Israel do so because they aspire to an elevated existence – a spiritual life rather than just a material one.

And so it is with power, which has a largely unrecognized spiritual dimension. Power conceived in mere material terms is just so much money or munitions, whereas the quality of being a superpower – a true superpower – goes beyond that. Really, it is to have God with you. Then it matters little how little you are. Then whatever one might possess is as nothing.

Because super power, as Zechariah 4:6 puts it, emanates from a source higher than the U.S., the U.N. or media talking heads:

"Not by strength and not by power, but by My spirit."

It's this spirit – found uniquely in the people of Israel, in the Land of Israel and in the Torah of Israel – that makes Israel's superpower future inevitable and close at hand.

Endnotes

1   http://www.pewforum.org/files/2015/11/201.11.03_RLS_II_full_report.pdf

2   http://www.pbs.org/wgbh/pages/frontline/dancingboys/
     http://www.nytimes.com/2015/09/21/world/asia/us-soldiers-told-to-ignore-afghan-allies-abuse-of-boys.html

3   http://www.meforum.org/4795/muslims-sexually-enslaving-children-a-global

4   http://www.israelnationalnews.com/Articles/Article.aspx/18115#.Vn-hKBV97WI

5   http://www.telegraph.co.uk/women/womens-life/11712599/Rotherham-paedophile-gangs-are-still-abusing-young-girls.html

6   http://quod.lib.umich.edu/p/ppotpus/4733017.1991.002?rgn=main;view=fulltext

7   http://www.gallup.com/poll/183413/americans-continue-shift-left-key-moral-issues.aspx

8   Quoted from http://www.yeshivaofkishinev.com/files/531_08%20-%20SIDRA%20KI%20SAY-TSAY%20-%20BATTLES%20AND%20MIRACLES%20AT%20WEST%20POINT%20ACADEMY.pdf.

9   http://www.defenseone.com/threats/2014/07/top-general-says-mexico-border-security-now-existential-threat-us/87958/

10   http://www.southcom.mil/newsroom/Documents/2014_SOUTHCOM_Posture_Statement_HASC_FINAL_PDF.pdf

11   http://www.scribd.com/doc/115962650/Global-Trends-2030-Alternative-Worlds

12   http://www.nytimes.com/2007/02/26/world/middleeast/26weapons.html?_r=0

13   http://www.nationalreview.com/article/427619/state-department-iran-deal-not-legally-binding-signed

14   http://www.telegraph.co.uk/news/worldnews/middleeast/iran/11729176/Iran-nuclear-deal-live.html

15   http://www.reuters.com/article/us-iran-missiles-usa-idUSKBN-0TR2G920151208

16   http://www.treasury.gov/resource-center/data-chart-center/Documents/20120413_FinancialCrisisResponse.pdf

17   http://www.bis.org/review/r081219c.pdf

18   http://nocamels.com/2015/09/multinational-high-tech-companies-presence-israel/

19   http://www.boi.gov.il/deptdata/mehkar/iser/01/iser_1.pdf

20   http://www.haaretz.com/news/jimmy-carter-israel-s-apartheid-policies-worse-than-south-africa-s-1.206865

21   http://www.timesofisrael.com/israeli-breakthrough-drug-helped-cure-jimmy-carters-cancer/

22   http://www.telegraph.co.uk/news/health/news/10713806/Just-two-in-five-people-offer-a-seat-to-the-frail-poll-finds.html

23   At least a third of Israeli restaurants are kosher, and the proportion is growing.

24   http://www.nrg.co.il/online/1/ART2/595/401.html

25   http://www.csmonitor.com/World/Middle-East/2015/0417/In-Israel-s-army-more-officers-are-now-religious.-What-that-means

26   http://www.haaretz.com/print-edition/features/why-does-the-idf-allow-officers-to-live-in-illegal-outposts-1.284991

27   http://www.avichai.org.il/sites/default/files/portrait-english-full-2009.pdf

28   http://uk.reuters.com/article/2015/11/16/uk-france-shooting-israel-sweden-idUKKCN0T523H20151116

29   http://www.israelnationalnews.com/News/News.aspx/191821#.VlMTSPkrLWI

30   https://www.youtube.com/watch?v=Ra879tN9pAA

31 http://pediatrics.aappublications.org/content/early/2014/06/25/peds.2013-2991

32 http://www.advocatesforyouth.org/publications/publications-a-z/413-adolescent-sexual-behavior-i-demographics

33 http://www.unodc.org/documents/data-and-analysis/WDR2012/WDR_2012_web_small.pdf

34 https://nccd.cdc.gov/youthonline/App/QuestionsOrLocations.aspx?CategoryId=C3

35 http://www.politico.com/story/2015/04/white-house-gender-neutral-bathroom-116779

36 http://www.buzzfeed.com/chrisgeidner/obama-administration-supports-transgender-student-in-federal?utm_   http://www.politico.com/story/2015/04/white-house-gender-neutral-bathroom-116779 term=.jmqp5BEPqz#.asqR5e1gaO

37 http://www.gallup.com/poll/183413/americans-continue-shift-left-key-moral-issues.aspx

38 https://blog.mozilla.org/blog/2014/04/03/brendan-eich-steps-down-as-mozilla-ceo/

39 http://articles.philly.com/2015-12-12/news/68963005_1_huckleberry-finn-n-word-central-school

40 http://www.campusreform.org/?ID=6946

41 http://www.meforum.org/2949/john-brennan-jihad-holy-struggle

42 http://georgewbush-whitehouse.archives.gov/news/releases/2001/09/20010917-11.html

43 http://www.bbc.com/news/world-middle-east-30041257

44 http://dailycaller.com/2015/11/19/obama-officials-trained-to-focus-on-behavior-not-religion-or-ideology/#ixzz3t3ckeLka

45 http://www.israelnationalnews.com/News/News.aspx/204176#.Vl1ik_krLWI

46 https://www.whitehouse.gov/the-press-office/2015/08/03/remarks-president-announcing-clean-power-plan

47 https://www.whitehouse.gov/the-press-office/2015/05/20/remarks-president-united-states-coast-guard-academy-commencement

48 http://www.reuters.com/article/2015/11/23/us-climatechange-summit-charles-idUSBN0TC0NO20151123#LEyFohYzEElVEAhi.99

49   http://www.telegraph.co.uk/comment/11367272/Climategate-the-sequel-How-we-are-STILL-being-tricked-with-flawed-data-on-global-warming.html

50   https://www.washingtonpost.com/news/post-politics/wp/2015/03/03/full-text-netanyahus-address-to-congress/

51   http://www.sfgate.com/business/article/FBI-Attack-on-PG-amp-E-substation-in-13-wasn-t-5746785.php

52   http://www.wsj.com/articles/pg-es-metcalf-substation-target-of-construction-equipment-theft-1409243813

53   http://www.mckinsey.com/global-themes/employment-and-growth/debt-and-not-much-deleveraging

54   McKinsey categorizes Israel as a developing country, but this seems to be a denial of reality, so we refer to it as advanced. (An experienced trader once told the author that the investment world has a financial stake in characterizing Israel as a developing economy, explaining that when the rest of the developing markets are imploding, portfolio managers can stash their money in Israeli investments and still fulfill their investment mandates while keeping the money safe.)

55   http://www.reuters.com/article/2013/03/30/us-cyprus-parliament-idUSBRE92G03I20130330#kiKp8pfhIlxTlPCs.97

56   http://www.reuters.com/article/2012/04/17/spain-argentina-ypf-idUSL2E8FHD9420120417

57   http://www.reuters.com/article/2013/07/17/us-argentina-chevron-idUSBRE96F18X20130717#f2go0JvLm7dMWHk3.97

58   http://www.wsj.com/articles/SB122721278056345271

59   http://www.ravaviner.com/2009/05/bar-kochba-from-then-until-now.html

60   http://www.aish.com/jl/jnj/jn/48929327.html

61   http://www.aish.com/sem/wp/Part_11_Monotheism_and_its_Implications.html

62   https://www.commentarymagazine.com/articles/arafat-and-the-uses-of-terror/

63   http://www.haaretz.com/news/report-rice-compares-life-in-u-s-south-to-palestinians-plight-1.234225

64   http://www.jpost.com/Diplomacy-and-Politics/Kerry-warns-if-peace-talks-fail-Israel-may-become-apartheid-state-350613

65   http://www.jpost.com/Operation-Protective-Edge/In-phone-call-to-Netanyahu-Obama-stresses-need-for-immediate-Gaza-cease-fire-369113

66   http://www.oxfordislamicstudies.com/Public/focus/essay1009_jefferson.html

67   https://www.whitehouse.gov/the-press-office/2015/11/16/press-conference-president-obama-antalya-turkey

68   http://www.prnewswire.com/news-releases/big-macr-beats-the-bible-for-majority-of-americans-ten-commandments-not-set-in-stone-58255387.html

69   http://jij.org/wp-content/uploads/2013/10/JIJ-Fact-Sheet-2-Money-Money-A4-Ver-11.pdf

70   http://www.meforum.org/4764/no-economic-aid-to-hamas-ruled-gaza

71   http://www.pewforum.org/files/2013/10/jewish-american-full-report-for-web.pdf

72   http://www.pewforum.org/files/2015/11/201.11.03_RLS_II_full_report.pdf

73   http://www.israelnationalnews.com/News/News.aspx/192627#.VmmD0Pl97WI

      http://www.israelhayom.com/site/newsletter_opinion.php?id=11681

74   http://www.nytimes.com/2015/03/06/us/debate-on-a-jewish-student-at-ucla.html?_r=0